# THE ANTICHRIST

✦ THE BARNES & NOBLE LIBRARY OF ESSENTIAL READING ✦

# THE ANTICHRIST
## A Criticism of Christianity

FRIEDRICH NIETZSCHE

TRANSLATED BY ANTHONY M. LUDOVICI

INTRODUCTION BY DENNIS SWEET

BARNES & NOBLE

NEW YORK

THE BARNES & NOBLE
LIBRARY OF ESSENTIAL READING

Introduction and Suggested Reading © 2006
by Barnes & Noble, Inc.

Originally published in 1895

This 2006 edition published by Barnes & Noble, Inc.

ISBN-13: 978-0-7607-7770-1
ISBN-10: 0-7607-7770-5

Printed and bound in the United States of America

3 5 7 9 10 8 6 4

# CONTENTS

# INTRODUCTION

"THIS BOOK BELONGS TO THE VERY FEW." SO BEGINS *THE ANTICHRIST*—
the most powerful and most bellicose criticism ever offered against
modern values and beliefs. The objects of these critiques are the
Christian Church and the Christian belief system. The "very few" to
whom the book is addressed are those "hyperboreans" who possess
"the courage for the *forbidden*"; those who "thirst for thunderbolts
and great deeds." The author and critic is Friedrich Nietzsche:
philosopher, psychologist, poet, and "the last disciple and initiate
of the god Dionysus." In earlier books Nietzsche had made that
most profound announcement: "God is dead." In other words, there
are no absolute, unconditional, or objective values in the world.
Whatever meanings that exist in life are put there by us, by human
beings, by "value-creators." *The Antichrist* was intended as the first
part of a four-part work to be titled *The Revaluation of All Values*—
Nietzsche's desire to lay bare the psychological, social, and cultural
weaknesses that humanity has imposed upon itself over the past two
thousand years, and to point to a higher sense of health and creative
development and responsibility for the future. An outline of this
proposed work provides the following scheme: (1) The Antichrist:
Attempt at a Critique of Christianity; (2) The Free Spirit: Critique of
Philosophy as a Nihilistic Movement; (3) The Immoralist: Critique
of the Most Fatal Kind of Ignorance, Morality; and (4) Dionysus:
Philosophy of Eternal Recurrence. *The Antichrist* is all that we have of
this ambitious enterprise, which was the last flash of creative frenzy
before Nietzsche's mind was dimmed by madness.

Friedrich Wilhelm Nietzsche was born in the village of Röcken in Saxony on October 15, 1844. His father, Karl Ludwig, was a Lutheran pastor who passed away when his son was only four years old, owing to "softening of the brain." Nietzsche and his younger sister, Elisabeth, were raised by their mother, Franziska, and their two maiden aunts. In 1858, he was admitted to the *Pfortaschule*, the most prestigious boarding school in Germany. After six years of the regimented life there, he spent a year as a theology student at the University of Bonn, then in 1865, he began the study of classical philology at the University of Leipzig. Nietzsche's literary career began with the publication in 1872 of *The Birth of Tragedy from the Spirit of Music*. The book's characterization of the creative impetus behind Greek drama in terms of a synthesis of the destructive "Dionysian" and the constructive "Apollinian" impulses, and its description of the Socratic attitude of reason over instinct as one of decadence, represents a seminal moment for the subsequent development of Nietzsche's thought. However, with its hyperbolic praise of his friend, the composer Richard Wagner (1813–83), the book did little to further Nietzsche's budding career as a professor of classical philology at Basel University in Switzerland. His friendship with Wagner, though, soon soured, and by 1878, they had become openly antagonistic toward one another. The following year Nietzsche resigned his teaching position at Basel, owing to the recurring health problems that plagued him throughout his life. These included severe eye pain and vision problems, intense headaches that would last for days, stomach and intestinal distress resulting in prolonged fits of vomiting, and chronic insomnia. Despite poor health and desperate loneliness, Nietzsche managed to produce a book (or a book-length supplement to an earlier publication) every year from 1878 to 1887. From 1883 to 1885, he published the four parts of his most famous work, *Thus Spoke Zarathustra*, in which he introduced his idea of the "overman" (*Übermensch*) and developed his conception of "the will to power" and his doctrine of "the eternal recurrence of the same." During the fall of 1888, in a flurry of energy and euphoria, Nietzsche wrote or completed four books: *Twilight of the Idols*, *The Antichrist*, *Ecce Homo*, and *Nietzsche Contra Wagner*. In early

January 1889, he collapsed in the street in Turin, Italy, confused and incoherent. He spent the last eleven years of his life institutionalized or under the care of his family.

Nietzsche's task, as he described it in *Ecce Homo*, his intellectual autobiography, was to uncover "the greatest uncleanliness that humanity has on its conscience; a self-deception become instinctive. . . . Blindness to Christianity is the crime par excellence— the crime against life." (*Ecce Homo*, IV, 7.) This was a task that he took very seriously.

> I know my fate. One day my name will be associated with the memory of something tremendous—a crisis without equal on earth, the most profound collision of conscience, a decision that was conjured up *against* everything that had been believed, demanded, hallowed so far. I am no man, I am dynamite. (*Ecce Homo*, IV, 1.)

The full force of this man made dynamite was Nietzsche's last and greatest undertaking: *The Revaluation of All Values*. In a letter dated October 18, 1888, to his friend Franz Overbeck, Nietzsche writes:

> It's my greatest harvest time. Everything comes easy now, everything I do thrives, although I think hardly anyone has ever undertaken such momentous things. That the first volume of the *Revaluation of All Values* is finished, ready for printing [i.e., *The Antichrist*]—I tell you this with a feeling I can't put into words. There'll be four books, appearing separately. This time, old artillery-man that I am, I'm moving in my big guns. I fear I'll be blasting the history of mankind into two halves. . . .
> (*Nietzsche: A Self-Portrait from His Letters*, 126.)

*The Antichrist* is not intended for the timid or the faint of heart. It seethes with contempt for what Nietzsche regards as mankind's greatest crime—Christianity's imposition, upon humanity, of its perverse and unnatural vision. Thematically the book stands with *Daybreak*, *Beyond Good and Evil*, *On the Genealogy of Morals*, and *Twilight of the Idols*. In each of these books Nietzsche had diagnosed Christian morality and values as the sources of our modern social and psychological maladies. Yet it is important to keep in mind that Nietzsche's criticisms are aimed at Christianity, understood as "organized religion," "the Christian Church," or, to use Kierkegaard's idiom, "Christiandom." Nietzsche makes this point in his notebooks: "What did Christ *deny?* Everything that is today called Christian" (*The Will to Power*, § 158.). In *The Antichrist* the point is made with a more pithy sentiment: "truth to tell, there never was more than one Christian, and he *died* on the Cross" (§ 39).

An analysis of the corrupting character of Christianity is the *modus operandi* of *The Antichrist*. Overall, the book is a negative, critical work. It was intended to clear the ground for the more positive discussions in the subsequent parts of *The Revaluation of All Values*. Nietzsche contends that the corruption here is manifold. First, the natural world and our instincts are sacrificed for a fantastic apparition dredged up by unhealthy imaginations. Second, the values offered, the ideals to which we aspire, are created by people who are not qualified to create such values and ideals. These meanings and goals are unnatural distortions of reality provided by people who are themselves divorced from reality, and who seek to instill in others the same dissatisfaction with this world which infects them. Thus, the priests and theologians create in others the same psychological distress and dis-integration from which they themselves suffer, and then proffer the cure. Third, the so-called source of the values and meanings of reality, the Christian God, represents, for Nietzsche, the low watermark in divine types. In the past, a people or culture created gods as expressions of its will to power, as manifestations of its abundance of creative energy. The Jewish God, Jehovah, was such an expression in its original conception as rainmaker and helper of the Jewish people. According to Nietzsche, later, after internal turmoil and external invasions, the Jewish priests "denaturalized" Jehovah, turning him into a moral world-orderer and judge.

In this context we find one of the great ironies that Nietzsche expresses so well. It has to do with the relationship between the God represented in Judaism and the God of Christianity. Despite his intolerance of anti-Jewish prejudices, some of Nietzsche's friends and acquaintances counted among the most notable anti-Semites of the period. These included Nietzsche's brother-in-law, Bernhard Förster, and, of course, Richard Wagner. Much of their rhetoric was spent in dissociating the "primitive" Jewish God of the Old Testament from the enlightened Christian God of the New Testament. Nietzsche contends that the Christian conception of God grew from the same soil as the Jewish conception, and that both are grounded in the same anti-natural attitudes of herd resentment. The difference consists in the fact that Judaism remained more or less exclusive to a single culture while Christianity opened the doors to every kind of disenfranchised group or belief system in the vastly diverse Roman Empire. Thus, Christianity "had to become as morbid, base and vulgar as the needs to which it had to minister were morbid, base and vulgar" (*The Antichrist*, § 37).

Despite its negative, critical tone, its thunder and its lightning, a rainbow does appear in *The Antichrist*. Here and elsewhere in his writings, Nietzsche's diagnosis of the Christian dis-ease is both an indictment of past crimes and an inducement for future virtues. Consider, for example, the virtue of pity. According to Nietzsche, the Christian conception of pity functions to drain the strength and the power of those who pity, and it serves to preserve the existence of those whom nature has, in many cases, written off. But there is another, healthier kind of pity, one that is grounded in an altogether different motive. In *Beyond Good and Evil*, he states the matter the following way:

> *Our* pity is a higher and more farsighted pity: we see how *man* makes himself smaller, how you make him smaller. . . . You want, if possible—and there is no more insane "if possible"—*to abolish suffering*. And we? It really seems that *we* would rather have it higher and

> worse than ever. . . . The discipline of suffering, of *great*
> suffering—do you not know that only *this* discipline has
> created all enhancements of man so far? (§ 225)

In *Thus Spoke Zarathustra*, Nietzsche draws a distinction between
degenerative virtues and motives, and the generative or *gift-giving*
motivation or virtue. While the former motives are grounded in
a kind of neurotic lack or need in a person's psyche, the latter
expresses itself in terms of an over-abundance of goodwill. It was the
gift-giving virtue that compelled Zarathustra to leave his cave after ten
years of solitary reflection and to "go under," i.e., to return to the realm
of human beings to share his wisdom: "like a bee that has gathered
too much honey; I need hands out-stretched to receive it. . . . Bless
the cup that wants to overflow, that the water may flow from it golden
and carry everywhere the reflection of your delight" (Zarathustra's
Prologue, 1). It is the gift-giving virtue that expresses the love that
the higher human has for his or her fellow human beings:

> Remain faithful to the earth, my brothers, with the power
> of your virtue. Let your gift-giving love and your knowl-
> edge serve the meaning of the earth. Thus I beg and
> beseech you. Do not let them fly away from earthly things
> and beat with their wings against eternal walls. . . . Lead
> back to the earth the virtue that flew away, as I do—back to
> the body, back to life, that it may give the earth a meaning,
> a human meaning. (*Thus Spoke Zarathustra*, I, 22, ii)

In *The Antichrist*, the motive is the same even if the voice is shriller and
the palliative is more caustic:

> Nothing is more unhealthy in the midst of our unhealthy
> modernity, than Christian pity. To be doctors *here*,
> to be inexorable *here*, to wield the knife effectively
> *here*—all this is our business, all this is *our* kind of love
> to *our* fellows, this is what makes *us* philosophers, us
> hyperboreans! (§ 7)

In Greek mythology, the Hyperboreans were separated from the world of men by a vast distance of space: they dwelled far to the north in an unknown realm of the world. Nietzsche's new Hyperboreans are (or will be) separated from his world by a vast distance of time. They are the philosophers of the future. His audience was, as yet, unborn. And as for the author himself: "Only the day after tomorrow belongs to me. Some are born posthumously" (*The Antichrist*, preface).

While some are born posthumously, Nietzsche's arrival in the twentieth century may be seen as a posthumous miscarriage. It is one of the saddest ironies in the history of ideas that his works were so misrepresented and misused by anti-Semites and by German nationalist organizations after his mental collapse. Nietzsche's position regarding the "German" nation, spirit, people, etc., is clear from his many reference to these subjects. After a moment of patriotic fervor during the Franco-Prussian War, he completely rejected Bismarck's expansionist policies and the attitudes that characterized the "new Germany" of the *zweite Reich*, as well as the idealized conception of the "good German." These views were clearly expressed, for example, in *Daybreak*, book 3; in *Beyond Good and Evil*, part 8, "Peoples and Fatherlands"; and in *Twilight of the Idols*, part 8, "What the Germans Lack." His criticism of the Germans is essentially criticism of the kind of sentimental, narrow-minded shallowness which he regarded as prevalent characteristics of German *Kultur* during the 1870s and 1880s. But there was a more sinister poison at work here as well, one that went hand in hand with the rise of German nationalism. This was the poison of anti-Semitism.

Nietzsche's views concerning the place and contribution of the Jews to German culture and to European culture in general were stated very well in his early aphoristic work, *Human, All Too Human*. These views never really changed.

> Incidentally, the whole problem of the *Jews* exists only within national states, inasmuch as their energy and higher intelligence, their capital of spirit and will, which accumulated from generation to generation in the long school of their suffering, must predominate to a degree that awakens envy and hatred; and so, in the literature of

nearly all present-day nations . . . there is an increase in the literary misconduct that leads the Jews to the slaughter-house, as scapegoats for every possible public and private misfortune. As soon as it is no longer a matter of preserving nations, but rather of producing the strongest possible mixed European race, the Jew becomes as useful and desirable an ingredient as any other national quantity (§ 475).

In this passage he continues to praise the Jewish people for having produced the noblest human being (Christ), the purest philosopher (Spinoza), the mightiest book (the Old Testament), and "the most effective moral code in the world." He further credits the Jews with having maintained the link between the world of antiquity and the world of the Enlightenment through the Dark Ages, via the Jewish educational system and the independent work of the Jewish academics. Even at the end of his career, at the onset of his madness, Nietzsche maintains his anti-anti-Semitism. In his last letter to his friend Jacob Burckhardt, dated January 5, 1889, he writes: "I've had Caiphas put in chains; I too was crucified last year in a long, drawn-out way by German doctors. Wilhelm, Bismarck, and all anti-Semites done away with!" (*Nietzsche: A Self-Portrait from His Letters*, 144).

Given this situation, it is indeed one of the most bizarre episodes of literary chicanery that Nietzsche's name would become associated with the Nazis; that he would become the philosopher of the Third Reich. How could such a thing happen? Certainly volumes have been written trying to shed light on this question. The short answer is this: Elisabeth Förster-Nietzsche. For most of her life Elisabeth was her brother's intimate confidant and supporter. However, in 1885, she married Bernhard Förster—a Berlin school teacher whose concerns about the influences of "international Jewry" led him to petition for the expulsion of Jews from the German stock exchange and, with Elisabeth, to found a "racially pure Aryan" colony, the "New Germany," in Paraguay. Although the colony failed and her husband committed suicide, Elisabeth's marriage and her right-wing politics appalled her brother and put a strain on their relationship that was never really reconciled. Sadly the recognition that Nietzsche pursued throughout his life only came after his mental breakdown. Subsequently, Elisabeth divided her time between attending to the colonists in Paraguay and taking care of her brother's business affairs, which included the publication in 1892 of a cheap collected edition of his works. In 1894, she established a Nietzsche Archive, which, in 1896, was moved to Weimar, where it is today.

As Walter Kaufmann makes clear in his seminal work on Nietzsche, in preparing her brother's manuscripts for publication in the various editions following his breakdown, Elisabeth was not averse to altering his manuscripts to suit her own social bias and political agenda. This included deleting passages as well as adding her own. She even completely withheld the publication of works until she thought that "the time was right" (e.g., *The Antichrist* [1895] and *Ecce Homo* [1908]). This is the beginning of the answer to the question, How did Nietzsche, who was so un-German and anti-anti-Semitic, become the philosophical poster boy for National Socialism? The version of Nietzsche that was presented to the public was distorted by the blatantly anti-Semitic, nationalistic predilections of his editor, his sister, Elisabeth. But she was not operating in a vacuum. By the end of the nineteenth century, anti-Semitism had been rehearsed by the historian J. A. Gobineau, espoused by Richard Wagner, and proclaimed as irrefutable truth by the political writer H. S. Chamberlain. Through the first few decades of the twentieth century the specter of anti-Jewish hatred was fermenting in much of Europe (and America). So too was the popularity of Nietzsche's thought. During World War I, for example, it was said that a copy of *Thus Spoke Zarathustra* was as essential as a shaving kit for the German soldier's rucksack.

With the advent of National Socialism, the lines regarding "the Jewish question" had been clearly drawn. But what the movement needed was some "objective" grounding. Dr. Hans F.K. Günther became the "scientific" foundation for the claims of Aryan superiority and Jewish decadence in the fields of history and anthropology. Hitler's *Mein Kampf* was the indisputable last word on the sociological aspects of "the Jewish question." What was needed was a bonafide philosophical foundation. Some of Hitler's more intellectually able cronies, including Alfred Rosenberg, thought that Nietzsche would be the obvious candidate. A second-rate writer and third-rate philosopher, Alfred Bäumler, was hired to interpret Nietzsche according to Nazi doctrine. At the entreaties of Elisabeth, Hitler visited the Nietzsche Archives in Weimar and posed with a bust of the philosopher. Thus was born the myth of Nietzsche as philosopher of the Third Reich.

Still, if Nietzsche was so vehemently against the German nationalistic spirit, and was so opposed to anti-Semitism, how is it possible, even with Elisabeth and her editor's red pencil, to so distort and modify his works such that even today many still regard him as a proto-Nazi racist? Certainly some of his doctrines, at first blush, do lend themselves to misinterpretation. This is partly a function of Nietzsche's intentionally unsystematic style, and partly a function of the intention to misrepresent him because of a political agenda. The discussions that come to mind here are (1) *the will to power*; (2) *the master-slave moralities*; and (3) *the "blond beast"* as mentioned here and there. As the "official" interpreter of Nietzsche's philosophy for the Third Reich, Bäumler's hermeneutic principles were fairly straightforward. First, one should ignore most of what Nietzsche said in his published works regarding Germans, Germany, and the Jews. Most of his bad feelings about Germany were said to be motivated by his disillusionment with Bismarck's politics, and should be overlooked. Most of his positive comments about the Jews were simply examples of his having been hoodwinked and deceived by these clever people. Second, to truly understand Nietzsche, we should, according to Bäumler, pay attention more or less exclusively to *The Will to Power* (1901–11)—Nietzsche's notes and drafts dating from 1883 to 1888, which his sister arranged and published after his death. These notes were never intended for publication; yet, according to Bäumler, they comprise a systematic presentation of views which are to be preferred over the views which the author published.

Bäumler's overall approach is too ludicrous to evoke criticism. However, with respect to the specific discussions mentioned above, the situation is much more complicated. (1) Nietzsche's doctrine of the will to power is about overcoming obstacles, about the strong dominating the weak, about power discharging itself and exploiting its environment. Yet to use this as a philosophical justification for invading Poland or for utilizing *Einsatzgruppen* to rid Ukrainian villages of undesirables is hardly justifiable. The expression of the will to power in the higher human being should be the expression of the domination of what is weakest in our nature by what is stronger; all under the eye of moderation and self-control and even benevolence to those weaker than ourselves. (2) The *master-slave moralities* were distinctions made in the second essay of Nietzsche's book, *On the Genealogy of Morals* (1887). It was a historical distinction having to do with the ancient civilizations of the Greeks and Romans. For the Nazis it seemed to imply that the Aryan/German civilization is intrinsically superior to other peoples/civilizations; and that, as the "master race," the Germans have the moral and legal sanctions to do whatever is necessary to maintain and flourish, regardless of the consequences for the "slave races." This kind of thinking was at the heart of Hitler's *Lebensraum* policy—his plan to invade the East, enslave the (employable) population, and colonize the land with Germans. However, Nietzsche's notion of master morality has nothing to do with any of this. For him, a master morality is one in which the individual creates his or her own values, and takes responsibility for them. Nothing could be further from this ideal than the automaton created by National Socialism. Furthermore, there is absolutely nothing racial in Nietzsche's conception of the master. Finally, (3) his occasional references to "the blond beast," were taken as clear evidence of his view of an ideal, blond-haired Nordic type. Yet when Nietzsche refers to "the blond beast," he employs the term as a metaphor to represent the unrestrained, unsublimated human instincts: a lion-like image that knows no racial bounds.

> One cannot fail to see at the bottom of all these noble races the beast of prey, the splendid *blond beast* prowling about avidly in search of spoil and victory; this hidden core needs to erupt from time to time, the animal has to get out again and go back to the wilderness: the Roman,

> Arabian, Germanic, Japanese nobility, the Homeric
> heroes, the Scandinavian Vikings—they all shared this
> need. (*On the Genealogy of Morals*, I, 11)

A final issue of interest and importance has to do with the eruption of
Nietzsche's own "hidden core," i.e., with his fall into insanity. There are
two questions here: First, what caused Nietzsche's madness? Second,
how did it begin to affect him? If such important works as *Twilight of
the Idols*, *The Antichrist*, and *Ecce Homo* were written or completed within
only a few months of his complete mental breakdown, might we not
suppose that these works show evidence of mental incompetence?

The cause of Nietzsche's insanity will, no doubt, always be a source
of speculation. Elisabeth, his sister, attributed his breakdown to an
over-indulgence in the various drugs he took for his plethora of
ailments (particularly his dependence upon chloral hydrate as a sleep-
inducer). Nietzsche's ex-confidant and "love" interest, Lou Salomé,
saw his condition as the inevitable outcome of his philosophical and
psychological questioning. Given the progressive nature of the loss of
his mental capacities, as well as the corresponding physical paralysis
that followed, the doctors who attended him during the final years
of his life described his condition as *dementia paralytica*. This is the
standard interpretation of Nietzsche's illness, the one that is prevalent today—that Nietzsche's madness was the result of the tertiary
stage of syphilis. One suggestion is that it was congenital syphilis,
contracted from his father, who had suffered from occasional seizures
and whose death was caused by "softening of the brain." This might
explain Nietzsche's own perpetual ill health from an early age, his
headaches that persisted for days, and his eye problems. Another
suggestion was provided by Nietzsche himself, immediately after the
inception of his madness. He informed his doctors that he had twice
infected himself at a brothel in 1866, while a student. The third
suggestion was that, in 1870, during his service as a medical orderly in
the Franco-Prussian War, Nietzsche had occasion to come into contact
with the blood of wounded soldiers, some of which may have been
infected with the syphilis bacteria.

Even though the syphilis explanation is the most widely accepted, it is not without its problems and its critics. The first suggestion, that Nietzsche contracted the disease from his father, has some time-frame problems. The second has a problem regarding the reliability of the source. He had, in a more lucid moment years earlier, described an "accidental" visit to a brothel. But he insisted that he sat and played the piano and did nothing more. The third option is usually entertained as the least implausible. But there are other possibilities. Over a year after his collapse, two of Nietzsche's closest friends, Peter Gast and Franz Overbeck, visited him on separate occasions and both came to the same conclusion regarding his condition: "it seemed—horrible though this is—as if Nietzsche were merely feigning madness, as if he were glad for it to have ended in this way" (Letter from Peter Gast to Carl Fuchs, January, 1890, quoted in Hayman, 341); "I cannot escape the ghastly suspicion . . . that his madness is simulated. This impression can be explained only by the experiences I have had of Nietzsche's self-concealments, of his spiritual masks" (letter from Franz Overbeck to his wife, February 24, 1890, Ibid.). Interestingly, nine years earlier Nietzsche had written:

> [A]ll superior men who were irresistibly drawn to throw
> off the yoke of any kind of morality and to frame new
> laws had, *if they were not actually mad,* no alternative
> but to make themselves or pretend to be mad. . . .
> Who would venture to take a look into the wilderness
> of bitterest and most superfluous agonies of soul in
> which probably the most fruitful men of all times
> have languished! To listen to the sighs of these soli-
> tary and agitated minds: "Ah, give me madness, you
> heavenly powers! Madness, that I may at last believe
> in myself! Give deliriums and convulsions, sudden
> lights and darkness, terrify me with frost and fire
> such as no mortal has ever felt, with deafening din
> and prowling figures, make me howl and whine and
> crawl like a beast: so that I may only come to believe

in myself! I am consumed by doubt, I have killed the law, the law anguishes me as a corpse does a living man: if I am not *more* than the law I am the vilest of men." (*Daybreak*, § 14)

Given the descriptions of Nietzsche's increasingly pathetic mental and physical deterioration over an eleven-year period, it seems completely absurd to regard Nietzsche's madness, as some have, as a conscious choice that he made in light of the overwhelming burden he assumed with the "revaluation of all values." It seems equally absurd to think that his madness was affected by him, and that he was not affected by the madness. But when and to what extent *was he affected*?

There were clear indications of what might be termed a profound lack of modesty in many of Nietzsche's correspondences beginning early in 1888; e.g., "Confidentially, it is not impossible that I am the foremost philosopher of this era, and perhaps even a little more, something decisive and ominous standing between two millennia." (Letter to Reinhard von Seydlitz, 12 February, 1888. *Nietzsche: A Self-Portrait from His Letters*, 106.) Such self-evaluation prefigures much of what he has to say of himself in his literary autobiography written later that year, *Ecce Homo*. That book is divided into four parts: "Why I Am So Wise"; "Why I Am So Clever"; "Why I Write Such Good Books"; and "Why I Am a Destiny." Are such pronouncements indications of Nietzsche's unbalanced mind? Certainly not, if one understands his contempt for the so-called "virtue" of modesty, and if one appreciates the scope of the task that he has undertaken.

Yet there are other indications that things are changing for Nietzsche. In his letters from October and November 1888, he speaks of how intensely he senses the world around him—of how spectacularly beautiful the streets of Turin are, of how tender the veal is, how succulent the grapes are, of how he eats four times as much as he used to. By December the intensity becomes delusional. He tells of how women stare at him in the streets, and of how he is treated as an exceptional person everywhere he goes (perhaps owing to the fact that he has given way to wearing, in public, a broad smirk or a tearful grimace). He insists that there is no longer any element of chance in his life, no coincidence. In a letter of December 18 to Carl Fuchs, he notes that "Everything is completed!" and that, "Since the old God has abdicated, *I* shall rule from now on" (*Nietzsche: A Self-Portrait from His Letters*, 137.). By this time he was signing his letters "Phoenix," "the Monster," and "Nietzsche Caesar."

On January 3, 1889, Nietzsche was walking down the Piazza Carlo Alberto in Turin when he observed a cab driver beating a horse. Tearfully, Nietzsche rushed over, embraced the horse around the neck, and collapsed in the street. This event is usually seen as the unambiguous inception of Nietzsche's madness. On the following day he wrote to his friend, Peter Gast: "To My Maestro Pietro—Sing me a new song: The world is transfigured and all the heavens are joyous. (Signed) The Crucified One" (*Nietzsche: A Self-Portrait from His Letters*, 141). The other letters and notes that follow have no real coherence whatsoever.

To condemn or to ignore any of Nietzsche's publications on the basis of the claim that they were the products of an unbalanced mind is to shortchange oneself of many valuable and interesting insights. His last works, including *The Antichrist*, were sometimes unpolished, occasionally vitriolic, and undeniably powerful. But a familiarity with his earlier works reveals an obvious organic development of the material and of Nietzsche's evaluation of his own value as a thinker and as a writer. Inhibitions are breaking down; not mental capacities.

**Dennis Sweet** holds a Ph.D. in philosophy from the University of Iowa. He writes frequently on Kant, Heraclitus, and Nietzsche, and teaches philosophy and history at several colleges in Pittsburgh.

# PREFACE

THIS BOOK BELONGS TO THE VERY FEW. MAYBE NOT ONE OF THEM
is yet alive; unless he be of those who understand my Zarathustra.
How *can* I confound myself with those who today already find a
hearing? Only the day after tomorrow belongs to me. Some are
born posthumously.

I am only too well aware of the conditions under which a man
understands me, and then *necessarily* understands. He must be intellectually upright to the point of hardness, in order even to endure my
seriousness and my passion. He must be used to living on mountain-
tops, and to feeling the wretched gabble of politics and national
egotism *beneath* him. He must have become indifferent; he must never
inquire whether truth is profitable or whether it may prove fatal. . . .
Possessing from strength a predilection for questions for which no
one has enough courage nowadays; the courage for the *forbidden;* his
predestination must be the labyrinth. The experience of seven soli-
tudes. New ears for new music. New eyes for the most remote things.
A new conscience for truths which hitherto have remained dumb. And
the will to economy on a large scale: to husband his strength and his
enthusiasm. . . . He must honor himself, he must love himself; he must
be absolutely free with regard to himself. . . . Very well then! Such men
alone are my readers, my proper readers, my preordained readers: of
what account are the rest? The rest are simply—humanity. One must
be superior to humanity in power, in loftiness of soul, in contempt.

FRIEDRICH NIETZSCHE

# THE ANTICHRIST

# THE ANTICHRIST

## 1

LET US LOOK EACH OTHER IN THE FACE. WE ARE HYPERBOREANS, we know well enough how far outside the crowd we stand. "Thou wilt find the way to the Hyperboreans neither by land nor by water": Pindar already knew this much about us. Beyond the north, the ice, and death—*our life, our happiness.* . . . We discovered happiness; we know the way; we found the way out of thousands of years of labyrinth. Who *else* would have found it? Not the modern man, surely? "I do not know where I am or what I am to do; I am everything that knows not where it is or what to do,"—sighs the modern man. We were made quite ill by *this* modernity, with its indolent peace, its cowardly compromise, and the whole of the virtuous filth of its Yea and Nay. This tolerance and *largeur de cœur* which "forgives" everything because it "understands" everything, is a Sirocco for us. We prefer to live amid ice than to be breathed upon by modern virtues and other southerly winds! . . . We were brave enough; we spared neither ourselves nor others: but we were very far from knowing whither to direct our bravery. We were becoming gloomy; people called us fatalists. *Our* fate—it was the abundance, the tension and the storing up of power. We thirsted for thunderbolts and great deeds; we kept at the most respectful distance from the joy of the weakling, from "resignation." . . . Thunder was in our air, that part of nature which we are, became overcast—*for we had no direction.* The formula of our happiness: a Yea, a Nay, a straight line, a goal.

2

What is good? All that enhances the feeling of power, the Will to Power, and power itself in man. What is bad? All that proceeds from weakness. What is happiness? The feeling that power is *increasing*, that resistance has been overcome.

Not contentment, but more power; not peace at any price, but war; not virtue, but efficiency[1] (virtue in the Renaissance sense, *virtù*, free from all moralic acid). The weak and the botched shall perish: first principle of our humanity. And they ought even to be helped to perish.

What is more harmful than any vice? Practical sympathy with all the botched and the weak Christianity.

3

The problem I set in this work is not what will replace mankind in the order of living beings (—Man is an *end*—); but, what type of man must be *reared*, must be *willed*, as having the highest value, as being the most worthy of life and the surest guarantee of the future.

This more valuable type has appeared often enough already: but as a happy accident, as an exception, never as *willed*. He has rather been precisely the most feared; hitherto he has been almost the terrible in itself; and from out the very fear he provoked there arose the will to rear the type which has now been reared, *attained:* the domestic animal, the gregarious animal, the sick animal man, the Christian.

4

Mankind does *not* represent a development towards a better, stronger or higher type, in the sense in which this is supposed to occur today. "Progress" is merely a modern idea—that is to say, a false idea.[2] The modern European is still far below the European of the Renaissance in value. The process of evolution does not by any means imply elevation, enhancement and increasing strength.

On the other hand isolated and individual cases are continually succeeding in different places on earth, as the outcome of the most different cultures, and in these a *higher type* certainly manifests itself: something which by the side of mankind in general, represents a kind of superman. Such lucky strokes of great success have always been possible and will perhaps always be possible. And even whole races, tribes and nations may in certain circumstances represent such *lucky strokes*.

5

We must not deck out and adorn Christianity: it has waged a deadly war upon this *higher* type of man, it has set a ban upon all the fundamental instincts of this type, and has distilled evil and the devil himself out of these instincts: the strong man as the typical pariah, the villain. Christianity has sided with everything weak, low, and botched; it has made an ideal out of *antagonism* towards all the self-preservative instincts of strong life: it has corrupted even the reason of the strongest intellects, by teaching that the highest values of intellectuality are sinful, misleading and full of temptations. The most lamentable example of this was the corruption of Pascal, who believed in the perversion of his reason through original sin, whereas it had only been perverted by his Christianity.

6

A painful and ghastly spectacle has just risen before my eyes. I tore down the curtain which concealed mankind's *corruption*. This word in my mouth is at least secure from the suspicion that it contains a moral charge against mankind. It is—I would fain emphasise this again—free from moralic acid: to such an extent is this so, that I am most thoroughly conscious of the corruption in question precisely in those quarters in which hitherto people have aspired with most determination to "virtue" and to "godliness." As you have already surmised, I understand corruption in the sense of *decadence*. What I maintain is this, that all the values upon which mankind builds its highest hopes and desires are *decadent* values.

I call an animal, a species, an individual corrupt, when it loses its instincts, when it selects and *prefers* that which is detrimental to it. A history of the "higher feelings," of "human ideals"—and it is not impossible that I shall have to write it—would almost explain why man is so corrupt. Life itself, to my mind, is nothing more nor less than the instinct of growth, of permanence, of accumulating forces, of power: where the will to power is lacking, degeneration sets in. My contention is that all the highest values of mankind *lack* this will, that the values of decline and of *nihilism* are exercising the sovereign power under the cover of the holiest names.

7

Christianity is called the religion of *pity*. Pity is opposed to the tonic passions which enhance the energy of the feeling of life: its action is depressing. A man loses power when he pities. By means of pity the drain on strength which suffering itself already introduces into the world is multiplied a thousandfold. Through pity, suffering itself becomes infectious; in certain circumstances it may lead to a total loss of life and vital energy, which is absurdly out of proportion to the magnitude of the cause (the case of the death of the Nazarene). This is the first standpoint; but there is a still more important one. Supposing one measures pity according to the value of the reactions it usually stimulates, its danger to life appears in a much more telling light. On the whole, pity thwarts the law of development which is the law of selection. It preserves that which is ripe for death, it fights in favor of the disinherited and the condemned of life; thanks to the multitude of abortions of all kinds which it maintains in life, it lends life itself a sombre and questionable aspect. People have dared to call pity a virtue (in every *noble* culture it is considered as a weakness); people went still further, they exalted it to *the* virtue, the root and origin of all virtues, but, of course, what must never be forgotten is the fact that this was done from the standpoint of a philosophy which was nihilistic, and on whose shield the device *The Denial of Life* was inscribed. Schopenhauer was right in this respect: by means of pity, life is denied and made *more worthy of denial,* pity is the *praxis* of Nihilism. I repeat, this depressing and infectious instinct thwarts those instincts which aim at the preservation and enhancement of the value life: by *multiplying* misery quite as much as by preserving all that is miserable, it is the principal agent in promoting decadence, pity exhorts people to nothing, to *nonentity!* But they do not say "*nonentity,*" they say "Beyond," or "God," or "the true life"; or Nirvana, or Salvation, or Blessedness, instead. This innocent rhetoric, which belongs to the realm of the religio-moral idiosyncrasy, immediately appears to be *very much less innocent* if one realizes what the tendency is which here tries to drape itself in the mantle of sublime expressions—the tendency of hostility to life. Schopenhauer was hostile to life: that is why he elevated pity to a virtue. . . . Aristotle, as you know, recognised in pity a morbid and dangerous state, of which it was wise to rid one's self from time to time by a purgative: he regarded tragedy as a purgative. For the sake of the instinct of life, it would certainly seem necessary to find some means of lancing any such morbid and dangerous accumulation of pity, as that which possessed Schopenhauer (and unfortunately the whole of our literary and artistic decadence as well, from St Petersburg to Paris, from Tolstoi to Wagner), if only to make it *burst.* . . . Nothing is more unhealthy in the midst of our unhealthy modernity, than Christian pity. To be doctors *here,* to be inexorable *here,* to wield the knife effectively *here,* all this is our business, all this is *our* kind of love to our fellows, this is what makes *us* philosophers, us hyperboreans!

8

It is necessary to state whom we regard as our antithesis: the theologians, and all those who have the blood of theologians in their veins—the whole of our philosophy. . . . A man must have had his very nose upon this fatality, or better still he must have experienced it in his own soul; he must almost have perished through it, in order to be unable to treat this matter lightly (the free-spiritedness of our friends the naturalists and physiologists is, in my opinion, a *joke,* what they lack in these questions is passion, what they lack is having suffered from these questions). This poisoning extends much further than people think: I unearthed the "arrogant" instinct of the theologian, wherever nowadays people feel themselves idealists, wherever, thanks to superior antecedents, they claim the right to rise above reality and to regard it with suspicion. . . . Like the priest the idealist has every grandiloquent concept in his hand (and not only in his hand!), he wields them all with kindly contempt against the "understanding," the "senses," "honors," "decent living," "science"; he regards such things as *beneath* him, as detrimental and seductive forces, upon the face of which, "the Spirit" moves in pure absoluteness: as if humility, chastity, poverty, in a word *holiness*, had not done incalculably more harm to life hitherto, than any sort of horror and vice. . . . Pure spirit is pure falsehood. . . . As long as the priest, the *professional* denier, calumniator and poisoner of life, is considered as the *highest* kind of man, there can be no answer to the question, what *is* truth? Truth has already been turned topsy-turvy, when the conscious advocate of nonentity and of denial passes as the representative of "truth."

9

It is upon this theological instinct that I wage war. I find traces of it everywhere. Whoever has the blood of theologians in his veins, stands from the start in a false and dishonest position to all things. The pathos which grows out of this state, is called *Faith:* that is to say, to shut one's eyes once and for all, in order not to suffer at the sight of incurable falsity. People convert this faulty view of all things into a moral, a virtue, a thing of holiness. They endow their distorted vision with a good conscience, they claim that no *other* point of view is any longer of value, once theirs has been made sacrosanct with the names "God," "Salvation," "Eternity." I unearthed the instinct of the theologian everywhere: it is the most universal, and actually the most subterranean form of falsity on earth. That which a theologian considers true, *must* of necessity be false: this furnishes almost the criterion of truth. It is his most profound self-preservative instinct which forbids reality ever to attain to honor in anyway, or even to raise its voice. Whithersoever the influence of the theologian extends, *valuations* are topsy-turvy, and the concepts "true" and "false" have necessarily changed places: that which is most deleterious to life, is here called "true," that which enhances it, elevates it, says Yea to it, justifies it and renders it triumphant, is called "false." . . . If it should happen that theologians, *via* the "conscience" either of princes or of the people, stretch out their hand for power, let us not be in any doubt as to what results therefrom each time, namely: the will to the end, the *nihilistic* will to power. . . .

10

Among Germans I am immediately understood when I say, that philosophy is ruined by the blood of theologians. The Protestant minister is the grandfather of German philosophy, Protestantism itself is the latter's *peccatum originale*. Definition of Protestantism: the partial paralysis of Christianity—and of reason. . . . One needs only to pronounce the words "Tübingen Seminary," in order to understand what German philosophy really is at bottom, i.e.,: theology *in disguise*. . . . The Swabians are the best liars in Germany, they lie innocently. . . . Whence came all the rejoicing with which the appearance of Kant was greeted by the scholastic world of Germany, three-quarters of which consist of clergymen's and schoolmasters' sons? Whence came the German conviction, which finds an echo even now, that Kant inaugurated a change for the *better?* The theologian's instinct in the German scholar divined what had once again been made possible. . . . A back-staircase leading into the old ideal was discovered, the concept "true world," the concept morality as the *essence* of the world (those two most vicious errors that have ever existed!), were, thanks to a subtle and wily scepticism, once again, if not demonstrable, at least no longer *refutable*. . . . Reason, the *prerogative* of reason, does not extend so far. . . . Out of reality they had made "appearance"; and an absolutely false world—that of being—had been declared to be reality. Kant's success is merely a theologian's success. Like Luther, and like Leibniz, Kant was one brake the more upon the already squeaky wheel of German uprightness.

11

One word more against Kant as a *moralist*. A virtue *must* be *our* invention, our most personal defence and need: in every other sense it is merely a danger. That which does not constitute a condition of our life, is merely harmful to it: to possess a virtue merely because one happens to respect the concept "virtue," as Kant would have us do, is pernicious. "Virtue," "Duty," "Goodness in itself," goodness stamped with the character of impersonality and universal validity—these things are mere mental hallucinations, in which decline the final devitalisation of life and Kœnigsbergian Chinadom find expression. The most fundamental laws of preservation and growth demand precisely the reverse, namely: that each should discover *his* own virtue, his own Categorical Imperative. A nation goes to the dogs when it confounds its concept of duty with the general concept of duty. Nothing is more profoundly, more thoroughly pernicious, than every impersonal feeling of duty, than every sacrifice to the Moloch of abstraction. Fancy no one's having thought Kant's Categorical Imperative *dangerous to life!* . . . The instinct of the theologist alone took it under its wing! An action stimulated by the instinct of life, is proved to be a proper action by the happiness that accompanies it: and that nihilist with the bowels of a Christian dogmatist regarded happiness as an *objection.* . . . What is there that destroys a man more speedily than to work, think, feel, as an automaton of "duty," without internal promptings, without a profound personal predilection, without joy? This is the recipe *par excellence* of decadence and even of idiocy. . . . Kant became an idiot. And he was the contemporary of Goethe! This fatal spider was regarded as *the* German philosopher, is still regarded as such! . . . I refrain from saying what I think of the Germans. . . . Did Kant not see in the French Revolution the transition of the State from the inorganic to the *organic* form? Did he not ask himself whether there was a single event on record which could be explained otherwise than as a moral faculty of mankind; so that by means of it, "mankind's tendency towards good," might be *proved* once and for all? Kant's reply: "that is the Revolution." Instinct at fault in anything and everything, hostility to nature as an instinct, German decadence made into philosophy *that is Kant!*

12

Except for a few sceptics, the respectable type in the history of philosophy, the rest do not know the very first pre-requisite of intellectual uprightness. They all behave like females, do these great enthusiasts and animal prodigies, they regard "beautiful feelings" themselves as arguments, the "heaving breast" as the bellows of divinity, and conviction as the *criterion* of truth. In the end, even Kant, with "Teutonic" innocence, tried to dress this lack of intellectual conscience up in a scientific garb by means of the concept "practical reason." He deliberately invented a kind of reason which at times would allow one to dispense with reason, that is to say when "morality," when the sublime command "thou shalt," makes itself heard. When one remembers that in almost all nations the philosopher is only a further development of the priestly type, this heirloom of priesthood, *this fraud towards one's self*, no longer surprises one. When a man has a holy life-task, as for instance to improve, save, or deliver mankind, when a man bears God in his breast, and is the mouthpiece of imperatives from another world, with such a mission he stands beyond the pale of all merely reasonable valuations. He is even sanctified by such a taste, and is already the type of a higher order! What does a priest care about science! He stands too high for that! And until now the priest has *ruled!* He it was who determined the concept "true and false."

13

Do not let us undervalue the fact that we *ourselves*, we free spirits, are already a "transvaluation of all values," an incarnate declaration of war against all the old concepts "true" and "untrue" and of a triumph over them. The most valuable standpoints are always the last to be found: but the most valuable standpoints are the methods. All the methods and the first principles of our modern scientific procedure, had for years to encounter the profoundest contempt: association with them meant exclusion from the society of decent people—one was regarded as an "enemy of God," as a scoffer at truth and as "one possessed." With one's scientific nature, one belonged to the Chandala. We have had the whole feeling of mankind against us; hitherto their notion of that which ought to be truth, of that which ought to serve the purpose of truth: every "thou shalt," has been directed against us. . . . Our objects, our practices, our calm, cautious distrustful manner—everything about us seemed to them absolutely despicable and beneath contempt. After all, it might be asked with some justice, whether the thing which kept mankind blindfold so long, were not an æsthetic taste: what they demanded of truth was a *picturesque* effect, and from the man of science what they expected was that he should make a forcible appeal to their senses. It was our *modesty* which ran counter to their taste so long. . . And oh! how well they guessed this, did these divine turkey-cocks!

## 14

We have altered our standpoint. In every respect we have become more modest. We no longer derive man from the "spirit," and from the "godhead"; we have thrust him back among the beasts. We regard him as the strongest animal, because he is the craftiest: one of the results thereof is his intellectuality. On the other hand we guard against the vain pretension, which even here would fain assert itself: that man is the great *arrière pensée* of organic evolution! He is by no means the crown of creation, beside him, every other creature stands at the same stage of perfection. . . . And even in asserting this we go a little too far; for, relatively speaking, man is the most botched and diseased of animals, and he has wandered furthest from his instincts. Be all this as it may, he is certainly the most *interesting!* As regards animals, Descartes was the first, with really admirable daring, to venture the thought that the beast was *machina,* and the whole of our physiology is endeavoring to prove this proposition. Moreover, logically we do not set man apart, as Descartes did: the extent to which man is understood today goes only so far as he has been understood mechanistically. Formerly man was given "free will," as his dowry from a higher sphere; nowadays we have robbed him even of will, in view of the fact that no such faculty is any longer known. The only purpose served by the old word "will," is to designate a result, a sort of individual reaction which necessarily follows upon a host of partly discordant and partly harmonious stimuli: the will no longer "effects" or "moves" anything. . . . Formerly people thought that man's consciousness, his "spirit," was a proof of his lofty origin, of his divinity. With the idea of perfecting man, he was conjured to draw his senses inside himself, after the manner of the tortoise, to cut off all relations with terrestrial things, and to divest himself of his mortal shell. Then the most important thing about him, the "pure spirit," would remain over. Even concerning these things we have improved our standpoint. Consciousness, "spirit," now seems to us rather a symptom of relative imperfection in the organism, as an experiment, a groping, a misapprehension, an affliction which absorbs an unnecessary quantity of nervous energy. We deny that anything can be done perfectly so long as it is done consciously. "Pure spirit" is a piece of "pure stupidity": if we discount the nervous system, the senses and the "mortal shell," we have miscalculated—that it is all! . . .

## 15

In Christianity, neither morality nor religion comes in touch at all with reality. Nothing but imaginary *causes* (God, the soul, the ego, spirit, free will—or even non-free will); nothing but imaginary *effects* (sin, salvation, grace, punishment, forgiveness of sins). Imaginary beings are supposed to have intercourse (God, spirits, souls); imaginary Natural History (anthropocentric: total lack of the notion "natural causes"); an imaginary *psychology* (nothing but misunderstandings of self, interpretations of pleasant or unpleasant general feelings; for instance of the states of the *nervus sympathicus*, with the help of the sign language of a religio-moral idiosyncrasy, repentance, pangs of conscience, the temptation of the devil, the presence of God); an imaginary teleology (the Kingdom of God, the Last Judgment, Everlasting Life). This purely fictitious world distinguishes itself very unfavorably from the world of dreams: the latter *reflects* reality, whereas the former falsifies, depreciates and denies it. Once the concept "nature" was taken to mean the opposite of the concept

God, the word "natural" had to acquire the meaning of abominable, the whole of that fictitious world takes its root in the hatred of nature (reality!), it is the expression of profound discomfiture in the presence of reality. . . . *But this explains everything.* What is the only kind of man who has reasons for wriggling out of reality by lies? The man who suffers from reality. But in order to suffer from reality one must be a bungled portion of it. The preponderance of pain over pleasure is the *cause* of that fictitious morality and religion: but any such preponderance furnishes the formula for decadence.

16

A criticism of the Christian concept of God inevitably leads to the same conclusion. A nation that still believes in itself, also has its own God. In him it honors the conditions which enable it to remain uppermost, that is to say, its virtues. It projects its joy over itself, its feeling of power, into a being, to whom it can be thankful for such things. He who is rich, will give of his riches: a proud people requires a God, unto whom it can *sacrifice* things. . . . Religion, when restricted to these principles, is a form of gratitude. A man is grateful for his own existence; for this he must have a God. Such a God must be able to benefit and to injure him, he must be able to act the friend and the foe. He must be esteemed for his good as well as for his evil qualities. The monstrous castration of a God by making him a God only of goodness, would lie beyond the pale of the desires of such a community. The evil God is just as urgently needed as the good God: for a people in such a form of society certainly does not owe its existence to toleration and humaneness. . . . What would be the good of a God who knew nothing of anger, revenge, envy, scorn, craft, and violence? Who had perhaps never experienced the rapturous *ardeurs* of victory and of annihilation? No one would understand such a God: why should one possess him? Of course, when a people is on the road to ruin; when it feels its belief in a future, its hope of freedom vanishing for ever; when it becomes conscious of submission as the most useful quality, and of the virtues of the submissive as self-preservative measures, then its God must also modify himself. He then becomes a tremulous and unassuming sneak; he counsels "peace of the soul," the cessation of all hatred, leniency and "love" even towards friend and foe. He is forever moralising, he crawls into the heart of every private virtue, becomes a God for everybody, he retires from active service and becomes a Cosmopolitan. . . . Formerly he represented a people, the strength of a people, everything aggressive and desirous of power lying concealed in the heart of a nation: now he is merely the good God. . . . In very truth Gods have no other alternative, they are *either* the Will to Power—in which case they are always the Gods of whole nations, or, on the other hand, the incapacity for power—in which case they necessarily become good.

## 17

Wherever the Will to Power, no matter in what form, begins to decline, a physiological retrogression, decadence, always supervenes. The godhead of *decadence*, shorn of its masculine virtues and passions is perforce converted into the God of the physiologically degraded, of the weak. Of course they do not call themselves the weak, they call themselves "the good." . . . No hint will be necessary to help you to understand at what moment in history the dualistic fiction of a good and an evil God first became possible. With the same instinct by which the subjugated reduce their God to "Goodness in itself," they also cancel the good qualities from their conquerer's God; they avenge themselves on their masters by diabolising the latter's God. The *good God* and the devil as well: both the abortions of decadence. How is it possible that we are still so indulgent towards the simplicity of Christian theologians today, as to declare with them that the evolution of the concept God, from the "God of Israel," the God of a people, to the Christian God, the quintessence of all goodness, marks a *step forward?* But even Renan does this. As if Renan had a right to simplicity! Why the very contrary stares one in the face. When the pre-requisites of *ascending* life, when everything strong, plucky, masterful and proud has been eliminated from the concept of God, and step by step he has sunk down to the symbol of a staff for the weary, of a last straw for all those who are drowning; when he becomes the pauper's God, the sinner's God, the sick man's God *par excellence*, and the attribute "Savior," "Redeemer," remains *over* as the one essential attribute of divinity: what does such a metamorphosis, such an abasement of the godhead imply? Undoubtedly, "the kingdom of God" has thus become larger. Formerly all he had was his people, his "chosen" people. Since then he has gone travelling over foreign lands, just as his people have done; since then he has never rested anywhere: until one day he felt at home everywhere, the Great Cosmopolitan, until he got the "greatest number," and half the world on his side. But the God of the "greatest number," the democrat among gods, did not become a proud heathen god notwithstanding: he remained a Jew, he remained the God of the back streets, the God of all dark corners and hovels, of all the unwholesome quarters of the world! . . . His universal empire is now as ever a netherworld empire, an infirmary, a subterranean empire, a ghetto-empire. . . . And he himself is so pale, so weak, so decadent. . . . Even the palest of the pale were able to master him—our friends the metaphysicians, those albinos of thought. They spun their webs around him so long that ultimately he was hypnotised by their movements and himself became a spider, a metaphysician. Thenceforward he once more began spinning the world out of his inner being—*sub specie Spinozæ*, thenceforward he transfigured himself into something ever thinner and ever more anæmic, became "ideal," became "pure spirit," became *"absolutum"* and "thing-in-itself." . . . *The decline and fall of a god:* God became the "thing-in-itself."

18

The Christian concept of God—God as the deity of the sick, God as a spider, God as spirit—is one of the most corrupt concepts of God that has ever been attained on earth. Maybe it represents the low-water mark in the evolutionary ebb of the godlike type. God degenerated into the *contradiction of life*, instead of being its transfiguration and eternal Yea! With God war is declared on life, nature, and the will to life! God is the formula for every calumny of this world and for every lie concerning a beyond! In God, nonentity is deified, and the will to nonentity is declared holy!

19

The fact that the strong races of Northern Europe did not repu-
diate the Christian God, certainly does not do any credit to their
religious power, not to speak of their taste. They ought to have been
able successfully to cope with such a morbid and decrepit offshoot
of decadence. And a curse lies on their heads; because they were
unable to cope with him: they made illness, decrepitude and contradiction a part of all their instincts, since then they have not *created*
any other God! Two thousand years have passed and not a single
new God! But still there exists, and as if by right, like an *ultimum*
and *maximum* of god-creating power, the *creator spiritus* in man, this
miserable God of Christian monotono-theism! This hybrid creature
of decay, nonentity, concept and contradiction, in which all the
instincts of decadence, all the cowardices and languors of the soul
find their sanction!

20

With my condemnation of Christianity I should not like to have done
an injustice to a religion which is related to it and the number of
whose followers is even greater; I refer to Buddhism. As nihilistic
religions, they are akin, they are religions of decadence, while
each is separated from the other in the most extraordinary fashion.
For being able to compare them at all, the critic of Christianity
is profoundly grateful to Indian scholars. Buddhism is a hundred
times more realistic than Christianity, it is part of its constitutional
heritage to be able to face problems objectively and coolly, it is
the outcome of centuries of lasting philosophical activity. The
concept "God" was already exploded when it appeared. Buddhism
is the only really *positive* religion to be found in history, even in its
epistemology (which is strict phenomenalism)—it no longer speaks
of the "struggle with *sin*" but fully recognising the true nature of
reality it speaks of the "struggle with *pain*." It already has—and this
distinguishes it fundamentally from Christianity, the self-deception
of moral concepts beneath it, to use my own phraseology, it stands

*Beyond Good and Evil.* The two physiological facts upon which it rests and upon which it bestows its attention are: in the first place excessive irritability of feeling, which manifests itself as a refined susceptibility to pain, *and also* as super-spiritualisation, an all-too-lengthy sojourn amid concepts and logical procedures, under the influence of which the personal instinct has suffered in favor of the "impersonal." (Both of these states will be known to a few of my readers, the objective ones, who, like myself, will know them from experience.) Thanks to these physiological conditions, a state of depression set in, which Buddha sought to combat by means of hygiene. Against it, he prescribes life in the open, a life of travel; moderation and careful choice in food; caution in regard to all intoxicating liquor, as also in regard to all the passions which tend to create bile and to heat the blood; and he deprecates care either on one's own or on other people's account. He recommends ideas that bring one either peace or good cheer, he invents means whereby the habit of contrary ideas may be lost. He understands goodness—being good—as promoting health. *Prayer* is out of the question, as is also *asceticism;* there is neither a Categorical Imperative nor any discipline whatsoever, even within the walls of a monastery (it is always possible to leave it if one wants to). All these things would have been only a means of accentuating the excessive irritability already referred to. Precisely on this account he does not exhort his followers to wage war upon those who do not share their views; nothing is more abhorred in his doctrine than the feeling of revenge, of aversion, and of resentment ("not through hostility doth hostility end": the touching refrain of the whole of Buddhism . . .). And in this he was right; for it is precisely these passions which are thoroughly unhealthy in view of the principal dietetic object. The mental fatigue which he finds already existent and which expresses itself in excessive "objectivity" (i.e., the enfeeblement of the individual's interest—loss of ballast and of "egoism"), he combats by leading the spiritual interests as well imperatively back to the individual. In Buddha's doctrine egoism is a duty: the thing which is above all necessary, i.e., "how canst thou be rid of suffering" regulates and defines the whole of the spiritual diet (let anyone but think of that Athenian who also declared war upon pure "scientificality," Socrates, who made a morality out of personal egoism even in the realm of problems).

21

The pre-requisites for Buddhism are a very mild climate, great gentleness and liberality in the customs of a people and *no* militarism. The movement must also originate among the higher and even learned classes. Cheerfulness, peace and absence of desire, are the highest of inspirations, and they are *realized*. Buddhism is not a religion in which perfection is merely aspired to: perfection is the normal case. In Christianity all the instincts of the subjugated and oppressed come to the fore: it is the lowest classes who seek their salvation in this religion. Here the pastime, the manner of killing time is to practise the casuistry of sin, self-criticism, and conscience inquisition. Here the ecstasy in the presence of a *powerful being*, called "god," is constantly maintained by means of prayer; while the highest thing is regarded as unattainable, as a gift, as an act of "grace." Here plain dealing is also entirely lacking: concealment and the darkened room are Christian. Here the body is despised, hygiene is repudiated as sensual; the church repudiates even cleanliness (the first Christian measure after the banishment of the Moors was the closing of the public baths, of which Cordova alone possessed 270). A certain spirit of cruelty towards one's self and others is also Christian: hatred of all those who do not share one's views; the will to persecute. Sombre and exciting ideas are in the foreground; the most coveted states and those which are endowed with the finest names, are really epileptic in their nature; diet is selected in such a way as to favor morbid symptoms and to over-excite the nerves. Christian, too, is the mortal hatred of the earth's rulers, the "noble,"—and at the same time a sort of concealed and secret competition with them (the subjugated leave the "body" to their master—all they want is the "soul"). Christian is the hatred of the intellect, of pride, of courage, freedom, intellectual *libertinage;* Christian is the hatred of the *senses*, of the joys of the senses, of joy in general.

22

When Christianity departed from its native soil, which consisted of the lowest classes, the *submerged masses* of the ancient world, and set forth in quest of power among barbaric nations, it no longer met with exhausted men but inwardly savage and self-lacerating men—the strong but bungled men. Here, dissatisfaction with one's self, suffering through one's self, is not as in the case of Buddhism, excessive irritability and susceptibility to pain, but rather, conversely, it is an inordinate desire for inflicting pain, for a discharge of the inner tension in hostile deeds and ideas. Christianity was in need of *barbaric* ideas and values, in order to be able to master barbarians: such are for instance, the sacrifice of the first-born, the drinking of blood at communion, the contempt of the intellect and of culture; torture in all its forms, sensual and non-sensual; the great pomp of the cult. Buddhism is a religion for *senile* men, for races which have become kind, gentle, and over-spiritual, and which feel pain too easily (Europe is not nearly ripe for it yet); it calls them back to peace and cheerfulness, to a regimen for the intellect, to a certain hardening of the body. Christianity aims at mastering *beasts of prey;* its expedient is to make them *ill,* to render feeble is the Christian recipe for taming, for "civilization." Buddhism is a religion for the close and exhaustion of civilization; Christianity does not even find civilization at hand when it appears, in certain circumstances it lays the foundation of civilization.

23

Buddhism, I repeat, is a hundred times colder, more truthful, more objective. It no longer requires to justify pain and its susceptibility to suffering by the interpretation of sin, it simply says what it thinks, "I suffer." To the barbarian, on the other hand, suffering in itself is not a respectable thing: in order to acknowledge to himself that he suffers, what he requires, in the first place, is an explanation (his instinct directs him more readily to deny his suffering, or to endure it in silence). In his case, the word "devil" was a blessing: man had an almighty and terrible enemy, he had no reason to be ashamed of suffering at the hands of such an enemy.

At bottom there are in Christianity one or two subtleties which belong to the Orient. In the first place it knows that it is a matter of indifference whether a thing be true or not; but that it is of the highest importance that it should be believed to be true. Truth and the belief that something is true: two totally separate worlds of interest, almost *opposite worlds*, the road to the one and the road to the other lie absolutely apart. To be initiated into this fact almost constitutes one a sage in the Orient: the Brahmins understood it thus, so did Plato, and so does every disciple of esoteric wisdom. If for example it give anyone pleasure to believe himself delivered from sin, it is *not* a necessary prerequisite thereto that he should be sinful, but only that he should *feel* sinful. If, however, *faith* is above all necessary, then reason, knowledge, and scientific research must be brought into evil repute: the road to truth becomes the *forbidden* road. Strong *hope* is a much greater stimulant of life than any single realized joy could be. Sufferers must be sustained by a hope which no actuality can contradict, and which cannot ever be realized: the hope of another world. (Precisely on account of this power that hope has of making the unhappy linger on, the Greeks regarded it as the evil of evils, as the most *mischievous* evil: it remained behind in Pandora's box.) In order that *love* may be possible, God must be a person. In order that the lowest instincts may also make their voices heard God must be young. For the ardor of the women a beautiful saint, and for the ardor of the men a Virgin Mary has to be pressed into the foreground. All this on condition that Christianity wishes to rule over a certain soil, on which Aphrodisiac or Adonis cults had already determined the *notion* of a cult. To insist upon *chastity* only intensifies the vehemence and profundity of the religious instinct—it makes the cult warmer, more enthusiastic, more soulful. Love is the state in which man sees things most widely different from what they are. The force of illusion reaches its zenith here, as likewise the sweetening and transfiguring power. When a man is in love he endures more than at other times; he submits to everything.

The thing was to discover a religion in which it was possible to love: by this means the worst in life is overcome—it is no longer even seen. So much for three Christian virtues Faith, Hope, and Charity: I call them the three Christian *precautionary measures*. Buddhism is too full of aged wisdom, too positivistic to be shrewd in this way.

24

Here I only touch upon the problem of the origin of Christianity. The first principle of its solution reads: Christianity can be understood only in relation to the soil out of which it grew, it is not a counter-movement against the Jewish instinct, it is the rational outcome of the latter, one step further in its appalling logic. In the formula of the Savior: "for Salvation is of the Jews." The second principle is: the psychological type of the Galilean is still recognisable, but it was only in a state of utter degeneration (which is at once a distortion and an overloading with foreign features) that he was able to serve the purpose for which he has been used, namely, as the type of a Redeemer of mankind.

The Jews are the most remarkable people in the history of the world, because when they were confronted with the question of Being or non-Being, with simply uncanny deliberateness, they preferred Being *at any price:* this price was the fundamental *falsification* of all Nature, all the naturalness and all the reality, of the inner quite as much as of the outer world. They hedged themselves in behind all those conditions under which hitherto a people has been able to live, has been allowed to live; of themselves they created an idea which was the reverse of *natural* conditions, each in turn, they twisted first religion, then the cult, then morality, history and psychology, about in a manner so perfectly hopeless that they were made *to contradict their natural value*. We meet with the same phenomena again, and exaggerated to an incalculable degree, although only as a copy: the Christian Church as compared with the "chosen people," lacks all claim to originality. Precisely on this account the Jews are the most *fatal* people in the history of the world: their ultimate influence has falsified mankind to such an extent, that even to this day the Christian can be anti-Semitic in spirit, without comprehending that he himself is the *final consequence of Judaism.*

It was in my "Genealogy of Morals" that I first gave a psychological exposition of the idea of the antithesis noble- and *resentment*-morality, the latter having arisen out of an attitude of negation to the former: but this is Judæo-Christian morality heart and soul. In order to be able to say Nay to everything that represents the ascending movement of life, prosperity, power, beauty, and self-affirmation on earth, the instinct of resentment, become genius, had to invent *another* world, from the standpoint of which that *Yea-saying* to life appeared as *the* most evil and most abominable thing. From the psychological standpoint the Jewish people are possessed of the toughest vitality. Transplanted amid impossible conditions, with profound self-preservative intelligence, it voluntarily took the side of all the instincts of decadence, *not* as though dominated by them, but because it detected a power in them by means of which it could assert itself *against* "the world." The Jews are the opposite of all *decadents:* they have been forced to represent them to the point of illusion, and with a *non plus ultra* of histrionic genius, they have known how to set themselves at the head of all decadent movements (St Paul and Christianity for instance), in order to create something from them which is stronger than every party *saying Yea to life.* For the category of men which aspires to power in Judaism and Christianity, that is to say, for the sacerdotal class, decadence is but a *means:* this category of men has a vital interest in making men sick, and in turning the notions "good" and "bad," "true" and "false," upside down in a manner which is not only dangerous to life, but also slanders it.

25

The history of Israel is invaluable as the typical history of every *denaturalisation* of natural values: let me point to five facts which relate thereto. Originally, and above all in the period of the kings, even Israel's attitude to all things was the *right* one—that is to say, the natural one. Its Jehovah was the expression of its consciousness of power, of its joy over itself, of its hope for itself: victory and salvation were expected from him, through him it was confident that Nature would give what a people requires—above all rain. Jehovah is the God of Israel, and *consequently* the God of justice: this is the reasoning of every people which is in the position of power, and which has a good conscience in that position. In the solemn cult both sides of this self-affirmation of a people find expression: it is grateful for the great strokes of fate by means of which it became uppermost; it is grateful for the regularity in the succession of the seasons and for all good fortune in the rearing of cattle and in the tilling of the soil. This state of affairs remained the ideal for some considerable time, even after it had been swept away in a deplorable manner by anarchy from within and the Assyrians from without. But the people still retained, as their highest desideratum, that vision of a king who was a good soldier and a severe judge; and he who retained it most of all was that typi-cal prophet (that is to say, critic and satirist of the age), Isaiah. But all hopes remained unrealized. The old God was no longer able to do what he had done formerly. He ought to have been dropped. What happened? The idea of him was changed, the idea of him was denaturalised: this was the price they paid for retaining him. Jehovah, the God of "Justice," is no longer one with Israel, no longer the expression of a people's sense of dignity: he is only a god on certain conditions. . . . The idea of him becomes a weapon in the hands of priestly agitators who henceforth interpret all happi-ness as a reward, all unhappiness as a punishment for disobedience to God, for "sin": that most fraudulent method of interpretation which arrives at a so-called "moral order of the Universe," by means of which the concept "cause" and "effect" is turned upside down. Once natural causation has been swept out of the world by reward and punishment, a causation *hostile to nature* becomes necessary; whereupon all the forms of unnaturalness follow. A God who *demands*, in the place of a God who helps, who advises, who is at bottom only a name for every happy inspiration of cour-age and of self-reliance. . . . Morality is no longer the expression of the conditions of life and growth, no longer the most fundamental instinct of life, but it has become abstract, it has become the opposite of life, Morality as the fundamental perversion of the imagination, as the "evil eye" for all things. What is Jewish morality, what is Christian morality? Chance robbed of its innocence; unhappiness polluted with the idea of "sin"; well-being interpreted as a danger, as a "temptation"; physiological indisposition poisoned by means of the canker-worm of conscience. . . .

26

The concept of God falsified; the concept of morality falsified: but the Jewish priesthood did not stop at this. No use could be made of the whole *history* of Israel, therefore it must go! These priests accomplished that miracle of falsification, of which the greater part of the Bible is the document: with unparalleled contempt and in the teeth of all tradition and historical facts, they interpreted their own people's past in a religious manner, that is to say, they converted it into a ridiculous mechanical process of salvation, on the principle that all sin against Jehovah led to punishment, and that all pious worship of Jehovah led to reward. We would feel this shameful act of historical falsification far more poignantly if the ecclesiastical interpretation of history through millenniums had not blunted almost all our sense for the demands of uprightness *in historicis*. And the church is seconded by the philosophers: *the lie* of "a moral order of the universe" permeates the whole development even of more modern philosophy. What does a "moral order of the universe" mean? That once and for all there is such a thing as a will of God which determines what man has to do and what he has to leave undone; that the value of a people or of an individual is measured according to how much or how little the one or the other obeys the will of God; that in the destinies of a people or of an individual, the will of God shows itself dominant, that is to say it punishes or rewards according to the degree of obedience. In the place of this miserable falsehood, *reality* says: a parasitical type of man, who can flourish only at the cost of all the healthy elements of life, the priest abuses the name of God: he calls that state of affairs in which the priest determines the value of things "the Kingdom of God"; he calls the means whereby such a state of affairs is attained or maintained, "the Will of God"; with cold-blooded cynicism he measures peoples, ages and individuals according to whether they favor or oppose the ascendancy of the priesthood. Watch him at work: in the hands of the Jewish priesthood the Augustan Age in the history of Israel became an age of decline; the exile, the protracted misfortune transformed itself into eternal *punishment* for the Augustan Age—that age in which the priest did not yet exist. Out of the mighty and thoroughly free-born figures of the history of Israel, they made, according to their require-ments, either wretched bigots and hypocrites, or "godless ones": they simplified the psychology of every great event to the idiotic formula "obedient or disobedient to God." A step further: the "Will of God," that is to say the self-preservative measures of the priesthood, must be known—to this end a "revelation" is necessary. In plain English: a stupendous literary fraud becomes necessary, "holy scriptures" are discovered, and they are published abroad with all hieratic pomp, with days of penance and lamentations over the long state of "sin." The "Will of God" has long stood firm: the whole of the trouble lies in the fact that the "Holy Scriptures" have been discarded. . . . Moses was already the "Will of God" revealed. . . . What had happened? With severity and pedantry, the priest had formulated once and for all—even to the largest and smallest contributions that were to be paid to him (—not forgetting the daintiest portions of meat; for the priest is a consumer of beef-steaks)—*what he wanted*, "what the Will of God was." . . . Henceforward everything became so arranged that the priests were *indispensable everywhere.* At all the natural events of life, at birth, at marriage, at the sick-bed, at death, not to speak of the sacrifice ("the meal"), the holy parasite appears in order to denatu-ralise, or in his language, to "sanctify," everything. . . . For this should be understood: every natural custom, every natural institution (the State, the administration of justice, marriage, the care of the sick and the poor), every demand inspired by the instinct of life, in short everything that has a value in itself, is rendered absolutely worthless and even dangerous through the parasitism of the priest (or of the "moral order of the universe"): a sanction after the fact is required, a *power which imparts value* is necessary, which in so doing says, Nay to nature, and which by this means alone *creates* a valuation. . . . The priest depreciates and desecrates nature: it is only at this price that he exists at all. Disobedience to God, that is to say, to the priest, to the "law," now receives the name of "sin"; the means of "reconciling one's self with God" are of course of a nature which render subordination to the priesthood all the more fundamental: the priest alone is able to "save." . . . From the psychological standpoint, in every society organised upon a hieratic basis, "sins" are indispensable: they are the actual weapons of power, the priest *lives* upon sins, it is necessary for him that people should "sin." . . . Supreme axiom: "God forgiveth him that repenteth"—in plain English: *him that submitteth himself to the priest.*

27

Christianity grew out of an utterly *false* soil, in which all nature, every natural value, every *reality* had the deepest instincts of the ruling class against it; it was a form of deadly hostility to reality which has never been surpassed. The "holy people" which had retained only priestly values and priestly names for all things, and which, with a logical consistency that is terrifying, had divorced itself from everything still powerful on earth as if it were "unholy," "worldly," "sinful,"—this people created a final formula for its instinct which was consistent to the point of self-suppression; as *Christianity* it denied even the last form of reality, the "holy people," the "chosen people," *Jewish* reality itself. The case is of supreme interest: the small insurrectionary movement christened with the name of Jesus of Nazareth, is the Jewish instinct *over again*, in other words, it is the sacerdotal instinct which can no longer endure the priest as a fact; it is the discovery of a kind of life even more fantastic than the one previously conceived, a vision of life which is even more unreal than that which the organisation of a church stipulates. Christianity denies the church.[3]

I fail to see against whom was directed the insurrection of which rightly or *wrongly* Jesus is understood to have been the promoter, if it were not directed against the Jewish church, the word "church" being used here in precisely the same sense in which it is used today. It was an insurrection against the "good and the just," against the "prophets of Israel," against the hierarchy of society—not against the latter's corruption, but against caste, privilege, order, formality. It was the lack of faith in "higher men," it was a "Nay" uttered against everything that was tinctured with the blood of priests and theologians. But the hierarchy which was set in question if only temporarily by this movement, formed the construction of piles upon which, alone, the Jewish people was able to subsist in the midst of the "waters"; it was that people's *last* chance of survival wrested from the world at enormous pains, the *residuum* of its political autonomy: to attack this construction was tantamount to attacking the most profound popular instinct, the most tenacious national will to live that has ever existed on earth. This saintly anarchist who called the lowest of the low, the outcasts and "sinners," the Chandala of Judaism, to revolt against the established order of things (and in language which, if the gospels are to be trusted, would get one sent to Siberia even today)—this man was a political criminal in so far as political criminals were possible in a community so absurdly non-political. This brought him to the cross: the proof of this is the inscription found thereon. He died for *his* sins—and no matter how often the contrary has been asserted there is absolutely nothing to show that he died for the sins of others.

28

As to whether he was conscious of this contrast, or whether he was merely *regarded* as such, is quite another question. And here, alone, do I touch upon the problem of the psychology of the Savior. I confess there are few books which I have as much difficulty in reading as the gospels. These difficulties are quite different from those which allowed the learned curiosity of the German mind to celebrate one of its most memorable triumphs. Many years have now elapsed since I, like every young scholar, with the sage conscientiousness of a refined philologist, relished the work of the incomparable Strauss. I was then twenty years of age; now I am too serious for that sort of thing. What do I care about the contradictions of "tradition"? How can saintly legends be called "tradition" at all! The stories of saints constitute the most ambiguous literature on earth: to apply the scientific method to them, *when there are no other documents to hand,* seems to me to be a fatal procedure from the start—simply learned fooling.

29

The point that concerns me is the psychological type of the Savior. This type might be contained in the gospels, in spite of the gospels, and however much it may have been mutilated, or overladen with foreign features: just as that of Francis of Assisi is contained in his legends in spite of his legends. It is *not* a question of the truth concerning what he has done, what he has said, and how he actually died; but whether his type may still be conceived in anyway, whether it has been handed down to us at all? The attempts which to my knowledge have been made to read the *history* of a "soul" out of the gospels, seem to me to point only to disreputable levity in psychological matters. M. Renan, that buffoon *in psychologicis,* has contributed the two most monstrous ideas imaginable to the explanation of the type of Jesus: the idea of the *genius* and the idea of the *hero* ("*héros*"). But if there is anything thoroughly unevangelical surely it is the idea of the hero. It is precisely the reverse of all struggle, of all consciousness of taking part in the fight, that has become instinctive here: the inability to resist is here converted into a morality ("resist not evil," the profoundest sentence in the whole of the gospels, their key in a certain sense), the blessedness of peace, of gentleness, of not *being able* to be an enemy. What is the meaning of "glad tidings"? True life, eternal life has been found—it is not promised, it is actually here, it is in *you;* it is life in love, in love free from all selection or exclusion, free from all distance. Everybody is the child of God—Jesus does not by any means claim anything for himself alone, as the child of God everybody is equal to everybody else. . . . Fancy making Jesus a *hero!* And what a tremendous misunderstanding the word "genius" is! Our whole idea of "spirit," which is a civilised idea, could have had no meaning whatever in the world in which Jesus lived. In the strict terms of the physiologist, a very different word ought to be used here. . . . We know of a condition of morbid irritability of the sense of *touch*, which recoils shuddering from every kind of contact, and from every attempt at grasping a solid object. Any such physiological *habitus* reduced to its ultimate logical conclusion, becomes an instinctive hatred of all reality, a flight into the "intangible," into the "incomprehensible"; a repugnance to all formulæ, to every notion of time and space, to everything that is established such as customs, institutions, the church; a feeling at one's ease in a world in which no sign of reality is any longer visible, a merely "inner" world, a "true" world, an "eternal" world. . . . "The Kingdom of God is within you." . . .

30

*The instinctive hatred of reality* is the outcome of an extreme susceptibility to pain and to irritation, which can no longer endure to be "touched" at all, because every sensation strikes too deep.

*The instinctive exclusion of all aversion, of all hostility, of all boundaries and distances in feeling,* is the outcome of an extreme susceptibility to pain and to irritation, which regards all resistance, all compulsory resistance as insufferable *anguish* (that is to say, as harmful, as *deprecated* by the self-preservative instinct), and which knows blessedness (happiness) only when it is no longer obliged to offer resistance to anybody, either evil or detrimental, love as the only ultimate possibility of life. . . .

These are the two *physiological realities* upon which and out of which the doctrine of salvation has grown. I call them a sublime further development of hedonism, upon a thoroughly morbid soil. Epicureanism, the pagan theory of salvation, even though it possessed a large proportion of Greek vitality and nervous energy, remains the most closely related to the above. Epicurus was a *typical* decadent: and I was the first to recognise him as such. The terror of pain, even of infinitely slight pain—such a state cannot possibly help culminating in a *religion* of love. . . .

31

I have given my reply to the problem in advance. The prerequisite thereto was the admission of the fact that the type of the Savior has reached us only in a very distorted form. This distortion in itself is extremely feasible: for many reasons a type of that kind could not be pure, whole, and free from additions. The environment in which this strange figure moved, must have left its mark upon him, and the history, the *destiny* of the first Christian communities must have done so to a still greater degree. Thanks to that destiny, the type must have been enriched retrospectively with features which can be interpreted only as serving the purposes of war and of propaganda. That strange and morbid world into which the gospels lead us—a world which seems to have been drawn from a Russian novel, where the scum and dross of society, diseases of the nerves and "childish" imbecility seem to have given each other rendezvous—must in any case have *coarsened* the: the first disciples especially must have translated an existence conceived entirely in symbols and abstractions into their own crudities, in order at least to be able to understand something about it, for them the type existed only after it had been cast in a more familiar mould. . . . The prophet, the Messiah, the future judge, the teacher of morals, the thaumaturgist, John the Baptist—all these were but so many opportunities of misunderstanding the type. . . . Finally, let us not underrate the *proprium* of all great and especially sectarian veneration: very often it effaces from the venerated object, all the original and frequently painfully unfamiliar traits and idiosyncrasies—*it does not even see them.* It is greatly to be deplored that no Dostoiewsky lived in the neighborhood of this most interesting decadent, I mean someone who would have known how to feel the poignant charm of such a mixture of the sublime, the morbid, and the childlike. Finally, the type, as an example of decadence, may actually have been extraordinarily multifarious and contradictory: this, as a possible alternative, is not to be altogether ignored. Albeit, everything seems to point away from it; for, precisely in this case, tradition would necessarily have been particularly true and objective: whereas we have reasons for assuming the reverse. Meanwhile a yawning chasm of contradiction separates the mountain, lake, and pastoral preacher, who strikes us as a Buddha on a soil only very slightly Hindu, from that combative fanatic, the mortal enemy of theologians and priests, whom Renan's malice has glorified as "*le grand maître en ironie.*" For my part, I do not doubt but what the greater part of this venom (and even of *esprit*) was inoculated into the type of the Master only as the outcome of the agitated condition of Christian propaganda. For we have ample reasons for knowing the unscrupulousness of all sectarians when they wish to contrive their own *apology* out of the person of their master. When the first Christian community required a discerning, wrangling, quarrelsome, malicious and hair-splitting theologian, to oppose other theologians, it created its "God" according to its needs; just as it did not hesitate to put upon his lips those utterly unevangelical ideas of "his second coming," the "last judgment,"—ideas with which it could not then dispense, and every kind of expectation and promise which happened to be current.

32

I can only repeat that I am opposed to the importation of the fanatic into the type of the Savior: the word "*impérieux,*" which Renan uses, in itself annuls the type. The "glad tidings" are simply that there are no longer any contradictions, that the Kingdom of Heaven is for the *children;* the faith which raises its voice here is not a faith that has been won by a struggle, it is to hand, it was there from the beginning, it is a sort of spiritual return to childishness. The case of delayed and undeveloped puberty in the organism, as the result of degeneration is at least familiar to physiologists. A faith of this sort does not show anger, it does not blame, neither does it defend itself: it does not bring "the sword," it has no inkling of how it will one day establish feuds between man and man. It does not demonstrate itself, either by miracles, or by reward and promises, or yet "through the scriptures": it is in itself at every moment its own miracle, its own reward, its own proof, its own "Kingdom of God." This faith cannot be formulated—it lives, it guards against formulæ. The accident of environment, of speech, of preparatory culture, certainly determines a particular series of conceptions: early Christianity deals only in Judæo-Semitic conceptions (the eating and drinking at the last supper form part of these, this idea which like everything Jewish has been abused so maliciously by the church). But one should guard against seeing anything more than a language of signs, semeiotics, an opportunity for parables in all this. The very fact that no word is to be taken literally, is the only condition on which this Anti-realist is able to speak at all. Among Indians he would have made use of the ideas of *Sankhyam*, among Chinese, those of *Lao-tze*—and would not have been aware of any difference. With a little terminological laxity Jesus might be called a "free spirit"—he cares not a jot for anything that is established: the word *killeth*, everything fixed *killeth*. The idea, *experience*, "life" as he alone knows it, is, according to him, opposed to every kind of word, formula, law, faith and dogma. He speaks only of the innermost things: "life" or "truth," or "light," is his expression for the innermost thing, everything else, the whole of reality, the whole of nature, language even, has only the value of a sign, of a simile for him. It is of paramount importance not to make any mistake at this point, however great may be the temptation thereto that lies in Christian—I mean to say, ecclesiastical prejudice. Any such essential symbolism stands beyond the pale of all religion, all notions of cult, all history, all natural science, all experience of the world, all knowledge, all politics, all psychology, all books and all Art—for his "wisdom" is precisely the complete ignorance[4] of the existence of such things. He has not even heard speak of *culture*, he does not require to oppose it, he does not deny it. . . . The same holds good of the state, of the whole of civil and social order, of work and of war—he never had any reason to deny the world, he had not the vaguest notion of the ecclesiastical concept "the world." . . . Denying is precisely what was quite impossible to him. Dialectic is also quite absent, as likewise the idea that any faith, any "truth" can be proved by argument (his proofs are inner "lights," inward feelings of happiness and self-affirmation, a host of "proofs of power"). Neither can such a doctrine contradict, it does not even realize the fact that there are or can be other doctrines, it is absolutely incapable of imagining a contrary judgment. . . .

Wherever it encounters such things, from a feeling of profound sympathy it bemoans such "blindness"—for it sees the "light"—but it raises no objections.

33

The whole psychology of the "gospels" lacks the concept of guilt and punishment, as also that of reward. "Sin," any sort of aloofness between God and man, is done away with, *this is precisely what constitutes the "glad tidings."* Eternal bliss is not promised, it is not bound up with certain conditions; it is the only reality—the rest consists only of signs wherewith to speak about it. . . .

The results of such a state project themselves into a new practice of life, the actual evangelical practice. It is not a "faith" which distinguishes the Christians: the Christian acts, he distinguishes himself by means of a *different* mode of action. He does not resist his enemy either by words or in his heart. He draws no distinction between foreigners and natives, between Jews and Gentiles ("the neighbor" really means the co-religionist, the Jew). He is angry with no one, he despises no one. He neither shows himself at the tribunals nor does he acknowledge any of their claims ("Swear not at all"). He never under any circumstances divorces his wife, even when her infidelity has been proved. All this is at bottom one principle, it is all the outcome of one instinct.

The life of the Savior was naught else than this practice, neither was his death. He no longer required any formulæ, any rites for his relations with God—not even prayer. He has done with all the Jewish teaching of repentance and of atonement; he alone knows the *mode* of life which makes one feel "divine," "saved," "evangelical," and at all times a "child of God." *Not* "repentance," *not* "prayer and forgiveness" are the roads to God: the *evangelical mode of life alone* leads to God, it *is* "God." That which the gospels abolished was the Judaism of the concepts "sin," "forgiveness of sin," "faith," "salvation through faith," the whole doctrine of the Jewish church was denied by the "glad tidings."

The profound instinct of how one must live in order to feel "in Heaven," in order to feel "eternal," while in every other respect one feels by *no* means "in Heaven": this alone is the psychological reality of "Salvation." A new life and *not* a new faith. . . .

34

If I understand anything at all about this great symbolist, it is this that he regarded only *inner* facts as facts, as "truths,"—that he understood the rest, everything natural, temporal, material and historical, only as signs, as opportunities for parables. The concept "the Son of Man," is not a concrete personality belonging to history, anything individual and isolated, but an "eternal" fact, a psychological symbol divorced from the concept of time. The same is true, and in the highest degree, of the *God* of this typical symbolist, of the "Kingdom of God," of the "Kingdom of Heaven," and of the "Sonship of God." Nothing is more un-Christlike than the *ecclesiastical crudity* of a personal God, of a Kingdom of God that is coming, of a "Kingdom of Heaven" beyond, of a "Son of God" as the second person of the Trinity. All this, if I may be forgiven the expression, is as fitting as a square peg in a round hole—and oh! What a hole! The gospels: a *world-historic* cynicism in the scorn of symbols. . . . But what is meant by the signs "Father" and "Son," is of course obvious—not to everybody, I admit: with the word "Son," *entrance* into the feeling of the general transfiguration of all things (beatitude) is expressed, with the word "Father," *this feeling itself,* the feeling of eternity and of perfection. I blush to have to remind you of what the Church has done with this symbolism: has it not set an Amphitryon story at the threshold of the Christian "faith"? And a dogma of immaculate conception into the bargain? . . . *But by so doing it defiled conception.*

The "Kingdom of Heaven" is a state of the heart—not something which exists "beyond this earth" or comes to you "after death." The whole idea of natural death is lacking in the gospels. Death is not a bridge, not a means of access: it is absent because it belongs to quite a different and merely apparent world the only use of which is to furnish signs, similes. The "hour of death" is not a Christian idea—the "hour," time in general, physical life and its crises do not exist for the messenger of "glad tidings." . . . The "Kingdom of God" is not something that is expected; it has no yesterday nor any day after tomorrow, it is not going to come in a "thousand years"—it is an experience of a human heart; it is everywhere, it is nowhere. . . .

35

This "messenger of glad tidings" died as he lived and as he taught— *not* in order "to save mankind," but in order to show how one ought to live. It was a mode of life that he bequeathed to mankind: his behavior before his judges, his attitude towards his executioners, his accusers, and all kinds of calumny and scorn, his demeanor on the *cross.* He offers no resistance; he does not defend his rights; he takes no step to ward off the most extreme consequences, he does more, he provokes them. And he prays, suffers and loves with those, in those, who treat him ill. . . . *Not* to defend one's self, *not* to show anger, not to hold anyone responsible. . . . But to refrain from resisting even the evil one, to *love* him. . . .

36

—Only we spirits that have *become free,* possess the necessary condition for understanding something which nineteen centuries have misunderstood, that honesty which has become an instinct and a passion in us, and which wages war upon the "holy lie" with even more vigor than upon every other lie. . . . Mankind was unspeakably far from our beneficent and cautious neutrality, from that discipline of the mind, which, alone, renders the solution of such strange and subtle things possible: at all times, with shameless egoism, all that people sought was their *own* advantage in these matters, the Church was built up out of contradiction to the gospel. . . .

Whoever might seek for signs pointing to the guiding fingers of an ironical deity behind the great comedy of existence, would find no small argument in the *huge note of interrogation* that is called

Christianity. The fact that mankind is on its knees before the reverse of that which formed the origin, the meaning and the *rights* of the gospel; the fact that, in the idea "Church," precisely that is pronounced holy which the "messenger of glad tidings" regarded as *beneath* him, as *behind* him—one might seek in vain for a more egregious example of *world-historic* irony.

37

—Our age is proud of its historical sense: how could it allow itself to be convinced of the nonsensical idea that at the beginning Christianity consisted only of the *clumsy fable of the thaumaturgist and of the Savior*, and that all its spiritual and symbolic side was only developed later? On the contrary: the history of Christianity—from the death on the cross onwards—is the history of a gradual and ever coarser misunderstanding of an original symbolism. With every extension of Christianity over ever larger and ruder masses, who were ever less able to grasp its first principles, the need of *vulgarising and barbarising* it increased proportionately—it absorbed the teachings and rites of all the *subterranean* cults of the *imperium Romanum*, as well as the nonsense of every kind of morbid reasoning. The fatal feature of Christianity lies in the necessary fact that its faith had to become as morbid, base and vulgar as the needs to which it had to minister were morbid, base and vulgar. *Morbid barbarism* at last braces itself together for power in the form of the Church—the Church, this deadly hostility to all honesty, to all loftiness of the soul, to all discipline of the mind, to all frank and kindly humanity. *Christian* and *noble* values: only we spirits *who have become free* have re-established this contrast in values which is the greatest that has ever existed on earth!

38

—I cannot, at this point, stifle a sigh. There are days when I am visited by a feeling blacker than the blackest melancholy—the *contempt of man*. And in order that I may leave you in no doubt as to what I despise, *whom* I despise: I declare that it is the man of today, the man with whom

I am fatally contemporaneous. The man of today, I am asphyxiated by his foul breath. . . . Towards the past, like all knights of knowledge, I am profoundly tolerant, that is to say, I exercise a sort of *generous* self-control: with gloomy caution I pass through whole millennia of this mad-house world, and whether it be called "Christianity," "Christian Faith," or "Christian Church," I take care not to hold mankind responsible for its mental disorders. But my feeling suddenly changes, and vents itself the moment I enter the modern age, *our* age. Our age *knows*. . . . That which formerly was merely morbid, is now positively indecent. It is indecent nowadays to be a Christian. *And it is here that my loathing begins.* I look about me: not a word of what was formerly known as "truth" has remained standing; we can no longer endure to hear a priest even pronounce the word "truth." Even he who makes but the most modest claims upon truth, *must* know at present, that a theologian, a priest, or a pope, not only errs but actually *lies*, with every word that he utters, and that he is no longer able to lie from "innocence," from "ignorance." Even the priest knows quite as well as everybody else does that there is no longer any "God," any "sinner" or any "Savior," and that "free will," and "a moral order of the universe" are *lies*. Seriousness, the profound self-conquest of the spirit no longer allows anyone to be *ignorant* about this. . . . All the concepts of the Church have been revealed in their true colors—that is to say, as the most vicious frauds on earth, calculated to *depreciate* nature and all natural values. The priest himself has been recognised as what he is—that is to say, as the most dangerous kind of parasite, as the actual venomous spider of existence. . . . At present we know, our *conscience* knows, the real value of the gruesome inventions which the priests and the Church have made, *and what end they served.* By means of them that state of self-profanation on the part of man has been attained, the sight of which makes one heave. The concepts "Beyond," "Last Judgment," "Immortality of the Soul," the "soul" itself, are merely so many instruments of torture, so many systems of cruelty, on the strength of which the priest became and remained master. . . . Everybody knows this, *and nevertheless everything remains as it was.* Whither has the last shred of decency, of self-respect gone, if nowadays even our statesmen—a body of men who are otherwise so unembarrassed, and such thorough anti-Christians in deed—still declare themselves Christians and still flock to communion?[5] . . . Fancy a prince at the head of his legions, magnificent as the expression of the egoism and self-exaltation of his people, but *shameless* enough to acknowledge himself a Christian! . . . What then does Christianity deny? What does it call "world"? "The world" to Christianity means that a man is a soldier, a judge, a patriot, that he defends himself, that he values his honor, that he desires his own advantage, that he is *proud*. . . . The conduct of every moment, every instinct, every valuation that leads to a deed, is at present anti-Christian: what an *abortion of falsehood* modern man must be, in order to be able *without a blush* still to call himself a Christian!

39

—I will retrace my steps, and will tell you the *genuine* history of Christianity. The very word "Christianity" is a misunderstanding, truth to tell, there never was more than one Christian, and he *died* on the Cross. The "gospel" *died* on the cross. That which thenceforward was called "gospel" was the reverse of that "gospel" that Christ had lived: it was "evil tidings," a *dysangel*. It is false to the point of nonsense to see in "faith," in the faith in salvation through Christ, the distinguishing trait of the Christian: the only thing that is Christian is the Christian mode of existence, a life such as he led who died on the Cross. . . . To this day a life of this kind is still possible; for certain men, it is even necessary: genuine, primitive Christianity will be possible in all ages. . . . *Not* a faith, but a course of action, above all a course of inaction, non-interference, and a different life. . . . States of consciousness, any sort of faith, a holding of certain things for true, as every psychologist knows, are indeed of absolutely no consequence, and are only of fifth-rate importance compared with the value of the instincts: more exactly, the whole concept of intellectual causality is false. To reduce the fact of being a Christian, or of Christianity, to a holding of something for true, to a mere phenomenon of consciousness, is tantamount to denying Christianity. *In fact there have never been any Christians.* The "Christian," he who for two thousand years has been called a Christian, is merely a psychological misunderstanding of self. Looked at more closely, there ruled in him, *notwithstanding* all his faith, only instincts—and *what instincts!* "Faith" in all ages, as for instance in the case of Luther, has always been merely a cloak, a pretext, a *screen*, behind which the instincts played their game, a prudent form of *blindness* in regard to the dominion of *certain* instincts. . . . "Faith" I have already characterised as a piece of really Christian cleverness; for people have always spoken of "faith" and acted according to their instincts. . . . In the Christian's world of ideas there is nothing which even touches reality: but I have already recognised in the instinctive hatred of reality the actual motive force, the only driving power at the root of Christianity. What follows therefrom? That here, even *in psychologicis*, error is fundamental, that is to say capable of determining the spirit of things, that is to say, *substance.* Take one idea away from the whole, and put one realistic fact in its stead, and the whole of Christianity tumbles into nonentity! Surveyed from above, this strangest of all facts, a religion not only dependent upon error, but inventive and showing signs of genius only in those errors which are dangerous and which poison life and the human heart—remains a *spectacle for gods*, for those gods who are at the same time philosophers and whom I met for instance in those celebrated dialogues on the island of Naxos. At the moment when they get rid of their *loathing* (—*and we do as well!*), they will be thankful for the spectacle the Christians have offered: the wretched little planet called Earth perhaps deserves on account of *this* curious case alone, a divine glance, and divine interest. . . . Let us not therefore underestimate the Christians: the Christian, false *to the point of innocence in falsity*, is far above the apes, in regard to the Christians a certain well-known theory of Descent becomes a mere good-natured compliment.

40

—The fate of the gospel was decided at the moment of the death, it hung on the "cross." . . . It was only death, this unexpected and ignominious death; it was only the cross which as a rule was reserved simply for the *canaille*, only this appalling paradox which confronted the disciples with the actual riddle: *Who was that? What was that?* The state produced by the excited and profoundly wounded feelings of these men, the suspicion that such a death might imply the *refutation* of their cause, and the terrible note of interrogation: "why precisely thus?" will be understood only too well. In this case everything *must* be necessary, everything must have meaning, a reason, the highest reason. The love of a disciple admits of no such thing as accident. Only then did the chasm yawn: "who has killed him?" "who was his natural enemy?"—this question rent the firmament like a flash of lightning. Reply: *dominant* Judaism, its ruling class. Thenceforward the disciple felt himself in revolt *against* established order; he understood Jesus, after the fact, as one in *revolt against established order*. Heretofore this warlike, this nay-saying and nay-doing feature in Christ had been lacking; nay more, he was its contradiction. The small primitive community had obviously understood *nothing* of the principal factor of all, which was the example of freedom and of superiority to every form of *resentment* which lay in this way of dying. And this shows how little they understood him altogether! At bottom Jesus could not have desired anything else by his death than to give the strongest public *example* and *proof* of his doctrine. . . . But his disciples were very far from *forgiving* this death—though if they had done so it would have been in the highest sense evangelical on their part, neither were they prepared, with a gentle and serene calmness of heart, to *offer* themselves for a similar death. . . . Precisely the most unevangelical feeling, *revenge*, became once more ascendant. It was impossible for the cause to end with this death: "compensation" and "judgment" were required (—and forsooth, what could be more unevangelical than "compensation," "punishment," "judgment"!) The popular expectation of a Messiah once more became prominent; attention was fixed upon one historical moment: the "Kingdom of God" descends to sit in judgment upon his enemies. But this proves that everything was misunderstood: the "Kingdom of God" regarded as the last scene of the last act, as a promise! But the Gospel had clearly been the living, the fulfilment, the *reality* of this "Kingdom of God." It was precisely a death such as Christ's that was this "Kingdom of God." It was only now that all the contempt for the Pharisees and the theologians, and all bitter feelings towards them, were introduced into the character of the Master, and by this means he himself was converted into a Pharisee and a theologian! On the other hand, the savage veneration of these completely unhinged souls could no longer endure that evangelical right of every man to be the child of God, which Jesus had taught: their revenge consisted in *elevating* Jesus in a manner devoid of all reason, and in separating him from themselves: just as, formerly, the Jews, with the view of revenging themselves on their enemies, separated themselves from their God, and placed him high above them. The Only God, and the Only Son of God: both were products of resentment.

## 41

—And from this time forward an absurd problem rose into prominence: "how *could* God allow it to happen?" To this question the disordered minds of the small community found a reply which in its absurdity was literally terrifying: God gave his Son as a *sacrifice* for the forgiveness of sins. Alas! How prompt and sudden was the end of the gospel! Expiatory sacrifice for guilt, and indeed in its most repulsive and barbaric form, the sacrifice of the *innocent* for the sins of the guilty! What appalling Paganism! For Jesus himself had done away with the concept "guilt,"—he denied any gulf between God and man, he *lived* this unity between God and man, it was this that constituted *his* "glad tidings." . . . And he did *not* teach it as a privilege! Thenceforward there was gradually imported into the type of the Savior the doctrine of the Last Judgment, and of the "second coming," the doctrine of sacrificial death, and the doctrine of *Resurrection*, by means of which the whole concept "blessedness," the entire and only reality of the gospel, is conjured away—in favor of a state *after* death! . . . St Paul, with that rabbinic impudence which characterises all his doings, rationalised this conception, this prostitution of a conception, as follows: "if Christ did not rise from the dead, our faith is vain." And, in a trice, the most contemptible of all unrealisable promises, the *impudent* doctrine of personal immortality, was woven out of the gospel. . . . St Paul even preached this immortality as a reward.

42

You now realize what it was that came to an end with the death on the cross: a new and thoroughly original effort towards a Buddhistic movement of peace, towards real and *not* merely promised *happiness on earth*. For, as I have already pointed out, this remains the fundamental difference between the two religions of *decadence:* Buddhism promises little but fulfils more, Christianity promises everything but fulfils nothing. The "glad tidings" were followed closely by the absolutely *worst* tidings—those of St Paul. Paul is the incarnation of a type which is the reverse of that of the Savior; he is the genius in hatred, in the standpoint of hatred, and in the relentless logic of hatred. And alas what did this dysangelist not sacrifice to his hatred! Above all the Savior himself: he nailed him to *his* cross. Christ's life, his example, his doctrine and death, the sense and the right of the gospel—not a vestige of all this was left, once this forger, prompted by his hatred, had understood in it only that which could serve his purpose. *Not* reality: *not* historical truth! . . . And once more, the sacerdotal instinct of the Jew, perpetrated the same great crime against history, he simply cancelled the yesterday, and the day before that, out of Christianity; he *contrived of his own accord a history of the birth of Christianity.* He did more: he once more falsified the history of Israel, so as to make it appear as a prologue to *his* mission: all the prophets had referred to *his* "Savior." . . . Later on the Church even distorted the history of mankind so as to convert it into a prelude to Christianity. . . . The type of the Savior, his teaching, his life, his death, the meaning of his death, even the sequel to his death—nothing remained untouched, nothing was left which even remotely resembled reality. St Paul simply transferred the centre of gravity of the whole of that great life, to a place *behind* this life, in the *lie* of the "resuscitated" Christ. At bottom, he had no possible use for the life of the Savior, he needed the death on the cross, *and* something more. To regard as honest a man like St Paul (a man whose home was the very headquarters of Stoical enlightenment) when he devises a proof of the continued existence of the Savior out of a hallucination; or even to believe him when he declares that he had this hallucination, would amount to foolishness on the part of a psychologist: St Paul desired the end, consequently he also desired the means. . . . Even what he himself did not believe, was believed in by the idiots among whom he spread *his* doctrine. What he wanted was power; with St Paul the priest again aspired to power, he could make use only of concepts, doctrines, symbols with which masses may be tyrannised over, and with which herds are formed. What was the only part of Christianity which was subsequently borrowed by Muhamed? St Paul's invention, his expedient for priestly tyranny and to the formation of herds: the belief in immortality—*that is to say, the doctrine of the "Last Judgment."* . . .

43

When the centre of gravity of life is laid, *not* in life, but in a beyond—*in nonentity*, life is utterly robbed of its balance. The great lie of personal immortality destroys all reason, all nature in the instincts, everything in the instincts that is beneficent, that promotes life and that is a guarantee of the future, henceforward aroused suspicion. The very meaning of life is now construed as the effort to live in such a way that life no longer has any point. . . . Why show any public spirit? Why be grateful for one's origin and one's forebears? Why collaborate with one's fellows, and be confident? Why be concerned about the general weal or strive after it? . . . All these things are merely so many "temptations," so many deviations from the "straight path." "One thing only is necessary." . . . That everybody, as an "immortal soul," should have equal rank, that in the totality of beings, the "salvation" of each individual may lay claim to eternal importance, that insignificant bigots and three-quarter-lunatics may have the right to suppose that the laws of nature may be persistently *broken* on their account, any such magnification of every kind of selfishness to infinity, to *insolence*, cannot be branded with sufficient contempt. And yet it is to this miserable flattery of personal vanity that Christianity owes its *triumph*, by this means it lured all the bungled and the botched, all revolting and revolted people, all abortions, the whole of the refuse and offal of humanity, over to its side. The "salvation of the soul"—in plain English: "the world revolves around me." . . . The poison of the doctrine *"equal* rights for all"—has been dispensed with the greatest thoroughness by Christianity: Christianity, prompted by the most secret recesses of bad instincts, has waged a deadly war upon all feeling of reverence and distance between man and man—that is to say, the *prerequisite* of all elevation, of every growth in culture; out of the resentment of the masses it wrought its *principal weapons* against us, against everything noble, joyful, exalted on earth, against our happiness on earth. . . . To grant "immortality" to every St Peter and St Paul, was the greatest, the most vicious outrage upon *noble* humanity that has ever been perpetrated. And do not let us underestimate the fatal influence which, springing from Christianity, has insinuated itself even into politics! Nowadays no one has the courage of special rights, of rights of dominion, of a feeling of self-respect and of respect for his equals, of *pathos of distance.* Our politics are diseased with this lack of courage! The aristocratic attitude of mind has been most thoroughly undermined by the lie of the equality of souls; and if the belief in the "privilege of the greatest number" creates and will continue *to create revolutions,* it is Christianity, let there be no doubt about it, and Christian values, which convert every revolution into blood and crime! Christianity is the revolt of all things that crawl on their bellies against everything that is lofty: the gospel of the "lowly" *lowers.* . . .

44

—The Gospels are invaluable as a testimony of the corruption which was already persistent *within* the first Christian communities. That which St Paul, with the logician's cynicism of a Rabbi, carried to its logical conclusion, was nevertheless merely the process of decay which began with the death of the Savior. These gospels cannot be read too cautiously; difficulties lurk behind every word they contain. I confess, and people will not take this amiss, that they are precisely on that account a joy of the first rank for a psychologist, as the reverse of all naïve perversity, as refinement *par excellence,* as a masterpiece of art in psychological corruption. The gospels stand alone. Altogether the Bible allows of no comparison. The *first* thing to be remembered if we do not wish to lose the scent here, is, that we are among Jews. The dissembling of holiness which, here, literally amounts to genius, and which has never been even approximately achieved elsewhere either by books or by men, this fraud in word and pose which in this book is elevated to an *Art*, is not the accident of any individual gift, of any exceptional nature. These qualities are a matter of *race*. With Christianity, the art of telling holy lies, which constitutes the whole of Judaism, reaches its final mastership, thanks to many centuries of Jewish and most thoroughly serious training and practice. The Christian, this *ultima ratio* of falsehood, is the Jew over again—he is even three times a Jew. . . . The fundamental will only to make use of concepts, symbols and poses, which are demonstrated by the practice of the priests, the instinctive repudiation of every other kind of practice, every other standpoint of valuation and of utility—all this is not only tradition, it is *hereditary:* only as an inheritance is it able to work like nature. The whole of mankind, the best brains, and even the best ages—(one man only excepted who is perhaps only a monster)—have allowed themselves to be deceived. The gospels were read as the *book of innocence* . . . this is no insignificant sign of the virtuosity with which deception has been practised here. Of course, if we could only succeed in seeing all these amazing bigots and pretended saints, even for a moment, all would be at an end—and it is precisely because *I* can read no single word of theirs, without seeing their pretentious poses, *that I have made an end of them.* . . . I cannot endure a certain way they have of casting their eyes heavenwards. Fortunately for Christianity, books are for the greatest number, merely *literature.* We must not let ourselves be led away: "judge not!" they say, but they dispatch all those to hell who stand in their way. Inasmuch as they let God do the judging, they themselves judge; inasmuch as they glorify God, they glorify themselves; inasmuch as they *exact* those virtues of which they themselves happen to be capable—nay more, of which they are in need in order to be able to remain on top at all; they assume the grand airs of struggling for virtue, of struggling for the dominion of virtue. "We live, we die, we sacrifice ourselves for the good" ("the Truth," "the Light," "the Kingdom of God"): as a matter of fact they do only what they cannot help doing. Like sneaks they have to play a humble part; sit away in corners, and remain obscurely in the shade, and they make all this appear a *duty:* their humble life now appears as a duty, and their humility is one proof the more of their piety. . . . Oh, what a humble, chaste and compassionate kind of falsity! "Virtue itself shall bear us testimony." . . . Only read the gospels as books calculated to seduce by means of morality: morality is appropriated by these petty people, they know what morality can do! The best way of leading mankind by the nose is with morality! The fact is that the most conscious *conceit* of people who believe themselves to be *chosen,* here simulates modesty: in this way they, the Christian community, the "good and the just" place themselves once and for all on a certain side, the side "of Truth"—and the rest of mankind, "the world" on the other. . . . This was the most fatal kind of megalomania that had ever yet existed on earth: insignificant little abortions of bigots and liars began to lay sole claim to the concepts "God," "Truth," "Light," "Spirit," "Love," "Wisdom," "Life," as if these things were, so to speak, synonyms of themselves, in order to fence themselves off from "the world"; little ultra-Jews, ripe for every kind of madhouse, twisted values round in order to suit themselves, just as if the Christian, alone, were the meaning, the salt, the standard and even the "*ultimate tribunal*" of all the rest of mankind. . . . The whole fatality was rendered possible only because a kind of megalomania, akin to this one and allied to it in race, the Jewish kind—was already to hand in the world: the very moment the gulf between Jews and Judæo-Christians was opened, the latter had no alternative left, but to adopt the same self-preservative measures as the Jewish instinct suggested, even *against* the Jews themselves, whereas the Jews, theretofore, had employed these same measures only against the Gentiles. The Christian is nothing more than an anarchical Jew.

45

—Let me give you a few examples of what these paltry people have stuffed into their heads, what they have laid *on the lips of their Master:* quite a host of confessions from "beautiful souls."

"And whosoever shall not receive you, nor hear you, when ye depart thence, shake off the dust under your feet for a testimony against them. Verily I say unto you, It shall be more tolerable for Sodom and Gomorrah in the day of judgment, than for that city." (Mark vi. 11.)—*How evangelical!* . . .

"And whosoever shall offend one of these little ones that believe in me, it is better for him that a millstone were hanged about his neck, and he were cast into the sea." (Mark ix. 42.)—How *evangelical!* . . .

"And if thine eye offend thee, pluck it out: it is better for thee to enter into the kingdom of God with one eye, than having two eyes to be cast into hell fire: where their worm dieth not, and the fire is not quenched." (Mark ix. 47, 48.)—The eye is not precisely what is meant in this passage. . . .

"Verily I say unto you, That there be some of them that stand here, which shall not taste of death, till they have seen the kingdom of God come with power." (Mark ix. 1.)—Well *lied*, lion![6] . . .

"Whosoever will come after me, let him deny himself, and take up his cross, and follow me. For . . ." (*A psychologist's comment.* Christian morality is refuted by its "For's": its "reasons" refute, this is Christian.) (Mark viii. 34.)

"Judge not, that ye be not judged. For with what judgment ye judge, ye shall be judged." (Matthew vii. 1, 2.)—What a strange notion of justice on the part of a "just" judge! . . .

"For if ye love them which love you, what reward have ye? Do not even the publicans the same? And if ye salute your brethren only, what do ye more *than others?* Do not even the publicans so?" (Matthew v. 46, 47.) The principle of "Christian love": it insists upon being *well paid.* . . .

"But if ye forgive not men their trespasses neither will your Father forgive your trespasses." (Matthew vi. 15.)—Very compromising for the "Father" in question.

"But seek ye first the kingdom of God, and his righteousness; and all these things shall be added unto you." (Matthew vi. 33.)— "All these things"—that is to say, food, clothing, all the necessities of life. To use a moderate expression, this is an *error.* . . . Shortly before this God appears as a tailor, at least in certain cases. . . .

"Rejoice ye in that day, and leap for joy: for, behold, your reward *is* great in heaven: for in the like manner did their fathers unto the prophets." (Luke vi. 23.)—*Impudent* rabble! They dare to compare themselves with the prophets. . . .

"Know ye not that ye are the temple of God and *that* the Spirit of God dwelleth in you? If any man defile the temple of God, *him shall God destroy;* for the temple of God is holy, which *temple ye are.*" (St Paul, 1 Corinthians iii. 16, 17.)—One cannot have too much contempt for this sort of thing. . . .

"Do ye not know that the saints shall judge the world? And if the world shall be judged by you, are ye unworthy to judge the smallest matters?" (St Paul, 1 Corinthians vi. 2.)—Unfortunately this is not merely the speech of a lunatic. . . . This *appalling impostor* proceeds thus: "Know ye not that we shall judge angels? How much more things that pertain to this life?"

"Hath not God made foolish the wisdom of this world? For after that in the wisdom of God, the world by wisdom knew not God, it pleased God by the foolishness of preaching to save them that believe . . . not many wise men after the flesh, not many mighty, not many noble *are called:* But God hath chosen the foolish things of the world to confound the wise; and God hath chosen the weak things of the world to confound the things which are mighty; And base things of the world, and things which are despised, hath God chosen; *yea,* and things which are not, to bring to nought things that are: That no flesh should glory in his presence." (St Paul, 1 Corinthians i. 20 *et seq.*)—In order to *understand* this passage, which is of the highest importance as an example of the psychology of every Chandala morality, the reader should refer to my *Genealogy of Morals:* in this book, the contrast between a *noble* and a Chandala morality born of *resentment* and impotent revengefulness, is brought to light for the first time. St Paul was the greatest of all the apostles of revenge. . . .

46

*What follows from this?* That one does well to put on one's gloves when reading the New Testament. The proximity of so much pitch almost defiles one. We should feel just as little inclined to hobnob with "the first Christians" as with Polish Jews: not that we need explain our objections. . . . They simply smell bad. In vain have I sought for a single sympathetic feature in the New Testament; there is not a trace of freedom, kindliness, open-heartedness and honesty to be found in it. Humaneness has not even made a start in this book, while *cleanly* instincts are entirely absent from it. . . . Only evil instincts are to be found in the New Testament, it shows no sign of courage, these people lack even the courage of their evil instincts. All is cowardice, all is a closing of one's eyes and self-deception. Every book becomes clean, after one has just read the New Testament: for instance, immediately after laying down St Paul, I read with particular delight that most charming and most wanton of scoffers, Petronius, of whom someone might say what Domenico Boccaccio wrote to the Duke of Parma about Cæsar Borgia: "*è tutto festo*"—immortally healthy, immortally cheerful and well-constituted. . . . These petty bigots err in their calculations and in the most important thing of all. They certainly attack; but everything they assail is, by that very fact alone, *distinguished*. He whom a "primitive Christian" attacks, is *not* thereby sullied. . . . Conversely it is an honor to be opposed by "primitive Christians." One cannot read the New Testament without feeling a preference for everything in it which is the subject of abuse—not to speak of the "wisdom of this world," which an impudent windbag tries in vain to confound "by the foolishness of preaching." Even the Pharisees and the Scribes derive advantage from such opposition: they must certainly have been worth something in order to have been hated in such a disreputable way. Hypocrisy—as if this were a reproach which the "first Christians" *were at liberty* to make! After all the Scribes and Pharisees were the *privileged ones:* this was quite enough, the hatred of the Chandala requires no other reasons. I very much fear that the "first Christian"—as also the "*last Christian*" *whom I may yet be able to meet,* is in his deepest instincts a rebel against everything privileged; he lives and struggles unremittingly for "equal rights"! . . . Regarded more closely, he has no alternative. . . . If one's desire be personally to represent "one of the chosen of God"—or a "temple of God," or "a judge of angels"—then every *other* principle of selection, for instance that based upon a standard of honesty, intellect, manliness and pride, or upon beauty and freedom of heart, becomes the "world"—*evil in itself.* Moral: every word on the lips of a "first Christian" is a lie, every action he does is an instinctive falsehood, all his values, all his aims are pernicious; but the man he hates, *the thing* he hates, *has value.* . . . The Christian, more particularly the Christian priest, is a *criterion of values*— Do I require to add that in the whole of the New Testament only *one* figure appears which we cannot help respecting? Pilate, the Roman Governor. To take a Jewish quarrel *seriously* was a thing he could not get himself to do. One Jew more or less—what did it matter? . . . The noble scorn of a Roman, in whose presence the word "truth" had been shamelessly abused, has enriched the New Testament with the only saying which *is of value,* and this saying is not only the criticism, but actually the shattering of that Testament: "What is truth!" . . .

47

—That which separates us from other people is not the fact that we can discover no God, either in history, or in nature, or behind nature, but that we regard what has been revered as "God," not as "divine," but as wretched, absurd, pernicious; not as an error, but as a *crime against life.* . . . We deny God as God. . . . If the existence of this Christian God were *proved* to us, we should feel even less able to believe in him. In a formula: *deus qualem Paulus creavit, dei negatio.* A religion such as Christianity which never once comes in touch with reality, and which collapses the very moment reality asserts its rights even on one single point, must naturally be a mortal enemy of the "wisdom of this world"—that is to say, *science.* It will call all those means good with which mental discipline, lucidity and severity in intellectual matters, nobility and freedom of the intellect may be poisoned, calumniated and *decried.* "Faith" as an imperative is a *veto* against science, *in praxi,* it means lies at any price. St Paul *understood* that falsehood—that "faith" was necessary; subsequently the Church understood St Paul. That "God" which St Paul invented for himself, a God who "confounds" the "wisdom of this world" (in a narrower sense, the two great opponents of all superstition, philology and medicine), means, in very truth, simply St Paul's firm *resolve* to do so: to call his own will "God", *thora*, that is arch-Jewish. St Paul insists upon confounding the "wisdom of this world": his enemies are the *good old* philologists and doctors of the Alexandrine schools; it is on them that he wages war. As a matter of fact no one is either a philologist or a doctor, who is not also an *Antichrist*. As a philologist, for instance, a man sees *behind* the "holy books," as a doctor he sees *behind* the physiological rottenness of the typical Christian. The doctor says "incurable," the philologist says "forgery."

48

—Has anybody ever really understood the celebrated story which stands at the beginning of the Bible, concerning God's deadly panic over *science*? . . . Nobody has understood it. This essentially sacerdotal book naturally begins with the great inner difficulty of the priest: *he* knows only one great danger, *consequently* "God" has only one great danger.

The old God, entirely "spirit," a high-priest through and through, and wholly perfect, is wandering in a leisurely fashion round his garden; but he is bored. Against boredom even the gods themselves struggle in vain.[7] What does he do? He invents man, man is entertaining. . . . But, behold, even man begins to be bored. God's compassion for the only form of misery which is peculiar to all paradises, exceeds all bounds: so forthwith he creates yet other animals. God's *first* mistake: man did not think animals entertaining, he dominated them, he did not even wish to be an "animal." Consequently God created woman. And boredom did indeed cease from that moment, but many other things ceased as well! Woman was God's *second* mistake. "Woman in her innermost nature is a serpent, Heva"—every priest knows this: "all evil came into this world through woman"—every priest knows this too. "*Consequently science* also comes from woman." . . . Only through woman did man learn to taste of the tree of knowledge. What had happened? Panic had seized the old God. Man himself had been his *greatest* mistake, he had created a rival for himself, science makes you *equal to God*, it is all up with priests and gods when man becomes scientific! Moral: science is the most prohibited thing of all, it alone, is forbidden. Science is the *first*, the germ of all sins, the original sin. *This alone is morality.* "Thou shalt *not* know": the rest follows as a matter of course. God's panic did not deprive him of his intelligence. How can one *guard* against science? For ages this was his principal problem. Reply: man must be kicked out of paradise! Happiness, leisure leads to thinking, all thoughts are bad thoughts. . . . Man *must* not think. And the "priest-per-se" proceeds to invent distress, death, the vital danger of pregnancy, every kind of misery, decrepitude, and affliction, and above all *disease,* all these are but weapons employed in the struggle with science! Trouble prevents man from thinking. . . . And notwithstanding all these precautions! Oh, horror! The work of science towers aloft, it storms heaven itself, it rings the death-knell of the gods, what's to be done? The old God invents *war;* he separates the nations, and contrives to make men destroy each other mutually (the priests have always been in need of war . . . ). War, among other things, is a great disturber of science! Incredible! Knowledge, *the rejection of the sacerdotal yoke,* nevertheless increases. So the old God arrives at this final decision: "Man has become scientific, *there is no help for it, he must be drowned!"* . . .

49

You have understood me. The beginning of the Bible contains the whole psychology of the priest. The priest knows only one great danger, and that is science, the healthy concept of cause and effect. But, on the whole, science flourishes only under happy conditions, a man must have time, he must also have superfluous mental energy in order to "pursue knowledge." . . . *"Consequently* man must be made unhappy"—this has been the argument of the priest of all ages. You have already divined what, in accordance with such a manner of arguing, must first have come into the world: "sin." . . . The notion of guilt and punishment, the whole "moral order of the universe," was invented against science, against the deliverance of man from the priest. . . . Man must *not* cast his glance upon the outer world, he must turn it inwards into himself; he must not as a learner look cleverly and cautiously *into* things; he must not see at all: he must *suffer*. . . . And he must suffer, so that he may be in need of the priest every minute. Away with doctors! What is needed is a Savior! The notion of guilt and punishment, including the doctrine of "grace," of "salvation" and of "forgiveness"—all *lies* through and through without a shred of psychological reality—were invented in order to destroy man's *sense of causality:* they are an attack on the concept of cause and effect! And *not* an attack with the fist, with the knife, with honesty in hate and love! But one actuated by the most cowardly, most crafty, and most ignoble instincts! A *priest's* attack! A *parasite's* attack! A vampyrism of pale subterranean leeches! . . . When the natural consequences of an act are no longer "natural," but are thought to be conjured up by phantom concepts of superstition, by "God," by "spirits," and by "souls," as merely moral consequences, in the form of rewards, punishments, hints, and educational means, then the whole basis of knowledge is destroyed, *then the greatest crime against man has been perpetrated.* Sin, I repeat, this form of self-pollution *par excellence* on the part of man, was invented in order to make science, culture and every elevation and noble trait in man quite impossible; by means of the invention of sin the priest is able to *rule.*

50

—I cannot here dispense with a psychology of "faith" and of the "faithful," which will naturally be to the advantage of the "faithful." If today there are still many who do not know how very *indecent* it is to be a "believer"—*or* to what extent such a state is the sign of decadence, and of the broken will to Life, they will know it no later than tomorrow. My voice can make even those hear who are hard of hearing. If perchance my ears have not deceived me, it seems that among Christians there is such a thing as a kind of criterion of truth, which is called "the proof of power." "Faith saveth; *therefore* it is true." It might be objected here that it is precisely salvation which is not proved but only *promised:* salvation is bound up with the condition "faith"—one *shall* be saved, *because* one has faith. . . . But how prove *that* that which the priest promises to the faithful really will take place, to wit: the "Beyond" which defies all demonstration? The assumed "proof of power" is at bottom once again only a belief in the fact that the effect which faith promises will not fail to take place. In a formula: "I believe that faith saveth; *consequently* it is true." But with this we are at the end of our tether. This "consequently" would be the *absurdum* itself as a criterion of truth. Let us be indulgent enough to assume, however, that salvation is proved by faith (*not* only desired, and *not* merely promised by the somewhat suspicious lips of a priest): could salvation—or, in technical terminology, *happiness*—ever be a proof of truth? So little is it so that, when pleasurable sensations make their influence felt in replying to the question "what is true," they furnish almost the contradiction of truth, or at any rate they make it in the highest degree suspicious. The proof through "happiness," is a proof of happiness—and nothing else; why in the world should we take it for granted that *true* judgments cause more pleasure than false ones, and that in accordance with a pre-established harmony, they necessarily bring pleasant feelings in their wake? The experience of all strict and profound minds teaches the *reverse.* Every inch of truth has been conquered only after a struggle, almost everything to which our heart, our love and our trust in life cleaves, has had to be sacrificed for it. Greatness of soul is necessary for this: the service of truth is the hardest of all services. What then is meant by honesty in things intellectual? It means that a man is severe towards his own heart, that he scorns "beautiful feelings," and that he makes a matter of conscience out of every Yea and Nay! Faith saveth: *consequently* it lies. . . .

51

The fact that faith may in certain circumstances save, the fact that salvation as the result of an *idée fixe* does not constitute a true idea, the fact that faith moves *no* mountains, but may very readily raise them where previously they did not exist—all these things are made sufficiently clear by a mere casual stroll through a *lunatic asylum.* Of course *no* priest would find this sufficient: for he instinctively denies that illness is illness or that lunatic asylums are lunatic asylums.

Christianity is in *need* of illness, just as Ancient Greece was in need of a superabundance of health. The actual ulterior motive of the whole of the Church's system of salvation is to *make people ill*. And is not the Church itself the Catholic madhouse as an ultimate ideal? The earth as a whole converted into a madhouse? The kind of religious man which the Church aims at producing is a typical *decadent*. The moment of time at which a religious crisis attains the ascendancy over a people, is always characterised by nerve-epidemics; the "inner world" of the religious man is ridiculously like the "inner world" of over-irritable and exhausted people; the "highest" states which Christianity holds up to mankind as the value of values, are epileptic in character, the Church has pronounced only madmen *or* great swindlers *in majorem dei honorem* holy. Once I ventured to characterise the whole of the Christian training of penance and salvation (which nowadays is best studied in England) as a *folie circulaire* methodically generated upon a soil which, of course, is already prepared for it, that is to say, which is thoroughly morbid. Not every one who likes can be a Christian: no man is "converted" to Christianity, he must be sick enough for it. . . . We others who possess enough courage both for health and for contempt, how rightly *we* may despise a religion which taught men to misunderstand the body! Which would not rid itself of the superstitions of the soul! Which made a virtue of taking inadequate nourishment! Which in health combats a sort of enemy, devil, temptation! Which persuaded itself that it was possible to bear a perfect soul about in a cadaverous body, and which, to this end, had to make up for itself a new concept of "perfection," a pale, sickly, idiotically gushing ideal, so-called "holiness"—holiness, which in itself is simply a symptom of an impoverished, enervated and incurably deteriorated body! . . . The movement of Christianity, as a European movement, was from first to last, a general accumulation of the ruck and scum of all sorts and kinds (and these, by means of Christianity, aspire to power). It does *not* express the downfall of a race, it is rather a conglomerate assembly of all the decadent elements from everywhere which seek each other and crowd together. It was not, as some believe, the corruption of antiquity, of *noble* antiquity, which made Christianity possible: the learned idiocy which nowadays tries to support such a notion cannot be too severely contradicted. At the time when the morbid and corrupted Chandala classes became Christianised in the whole of the *imperium*, the very *contrary type*, nobility, was extant in its finest and maturest forms. The greatest number became master; the democracy of Christian instincts triumphed. . . . Christianity was not "national," it was not determined by race, it appealed to all the disinherited forms of life, it had its allies everywhere. Christianity is built upon the rancour of the sick; its instinct is directed *against* the sound, against health. Everything well-constituted, proud, high-spirited, and beautiful is offensive to its ears and eyes. Again I remind you of St Paul's priceless words: "And God hath chosen the *weak* things of the world, the *foolish* things of the world; and *base* things of the world, and things which are *despised*": this was the formula, *in hoc signo* decadence triumphed. *God on the Cross*—does no one yet understand the terrible ulterior motive of this symbol? Everything that suffers, everything that hangs on the cross, is *divine*. . . . All of us hang on the cross, consequently we are *divine*. . . . We alone are divine. . . . Christianity was a victory; a *nobler* type of character perished through it, Christianity has been humanity's greatest misfortune hitherto.

52

Christianity also stands opposed to everything happily constituted in the *mind*, it can make use only of morbid reason as Christian reason; it takes the side of everything idiotic, it utters a curse upon "intellect," upon the *superbia* of the healthy intellect. Since illness belongs to the essence of Christianity, the typically Christian state, "faith," *must* also be a form of illness, and all straight, honest and scientific roads to knowledge must be repudiated by the Church as forbidden. . . . Doubt in itself is already a sin. . . . The total lack of psychological cleanliness in the priest, which reveals itself in his look, is a *result* of decadence. Hysterical women, as also children with scrofulous constitutions, should be observed as a proof of how invariably instinctive falsity, the love of lying for the sake of lying, and the inability either to look or to walk straight, are the expression of decadence. "Faith" simply means the refusal to know what is true. The pious person, the priest of both sexes, is false because he is ill: his instinct *demands* that truth should not assert its right anywhere. "That which makes ill is good: that which proceeds from abundance, from superabundance and from power, is evil": that is the view of the faithful. The *constraint to lie*—that is the sign by which I recognise every predetermined theologian. Another characteristic of the theologian is his lack of *capacity* for *philology*. What I mean here by the word philology is, in a general sense to be understood as the art of reading well, of being able to take account of facts *without* falsifying them by interpretation, without losing either caution, patience or subtlety owing to one's desire to understand. Philology as *ephexis*[8] in interpretation, whether one be dealing with books, newspaper reports, human destinies or meteorological records, not to speak of the "salvation of the soul." . . . The manner in which a theologian, whether in Berlin or in Rome, interprets a verse from the "Scriptures," or an experience, or the triumph of his nation's army for instance, under the superior guiding light of David's Psalms, is always so exceedingly *daring*, that it is enough to make a philologist's hair stand on end. And what is he to do, when pietists and other cows from Swabia explain their miserable everyday lives in their smoky hovels by means of the "Finger of God," a miracle of "grace," of "Providence," of experiences of "salvation"! The most modest effort of the intellect, not to speak of decent feeling, ought at least to lead these interpreters to convince themselves of the absolute childishness and unworthiness of any such abuse of the dexterity of God's fingers. However small an amount of loving piety we might possess, a god who cured us in time of a cold in the nose, or who arranged for us to enter a carriage just at the moment when a cloud burst over our heads, would be such an absurd God, that he would have to be abolished, even if he existed.[9] God as a domestic servant, as a postman, as a general provider, in short, merely a word for the most foolish kind of accidents. . . . "Divine Providence," as it is believed in today by almost every third man in "cultured Germany," would be an argument against God, in fact it would be the strongest argument against God that could be imagined. And in any case it is an argument against the Germans.

53

—The notion that martyrs prove anything at all in favor of a thing, is so exceedingly doubtful, that I would fain deny that there has ever yet existed a martyr who had anything to do with truth. In the very manner in which a martyr flings his little parcel of truth at the head of the world, such a low degree of intellectual honesty and such obtuseness in regard to the question "truth" makes itself felt, that one never requires to refute a martyr. Truth is not a thing which one might have and another be without: only peasants or peasant-apostles, after the style of Luther, can think like this about truth. You may be quite sure, that the greater a man's degree of conscientiousness may be in matters intellectual, the more modest he will show himself on this point. To *know* about five things, and with a subtle wave of the hand to refuse to know *others*. . . . "Truth" as it is understood by every prophet, every sectarian, every free thinker, every social-ist and every churchman, is an absolute proof of the fact that these people haven't even begun that discipline of the mind and that process of self-mastery, which is necessary for the discovery of any small, even exceedingly small truth. Incidentally, the deaths of martyrs have been a great misfortune in the history of the world: they led people astray. . . . The conclusion which all idiots, women and common people come to, that there must be something in a cause for which someone lays down his life (or which, as in the case of primitive Christianity, provokes an epidemic of sacrifices), this conclusion put a tremendous check upon all investigation, upon the spirit of investigation and of caution. Martyrs have *harmed* the cause of truth. . . . Even to this day it only requires the crude fact of persecution, in order to create an honorable name for any obscure sect who does not matter in the least. What? Is a cause actually changed in anyway by the fact that someone has laid down his life for it? An error which becomes honorable, is simply an error that possesses one seductive charm the more: do you suppose, dear theologians, that we shall give you the chance of acting the martyrs for your lies? A thing is refuted by being laid respectfully on ice, and theologians are refuted in the same way. This was precisely the world-historic foolishness of all persecutors; they lent the thing they combated a semblance of honor by conferring the fascination of martyrdom upon it. . . . Women still lie prostrate before an error today, because they have been told that someone died on the cross for it. *Is the cross then an argument?* But concerning all these things, one person alone has said what mankind has been in need of for thousands of years, *Zarathustra*.

"Letters of blood did they write on the way they went, and their folly taught that truth is proved by blood.

"But blood is the very worst testimony of truth; blood poisoneth even the purest teaching, and turneth it into delusion and into blood feuds.

"And when a man goeth through fire for his teaching—what does that prove? Verily, it is more when out of one's own burning springeth one's own teaching."[10]

54

Do not allow yourselves to be deceived: great minds are sceptical. Zarathustra is a sceptic. Strength and the *freedom* which proceeds from the power and excessive power of the mind, *manifests* itself through scepticism. Men of conviction are of no account whatever in regard to any principles of value or of non-value. Convictions are prisons. They never see far enough, they do not look down from a sufficient height: but in order to have any say in questions of value and non-value, a man must see five hundred convictions *beneath* him, *behind* him. . . . A spirit who desires great things, and who also desires the means thereto, is necessarily a sceptic. Freedom from every kind of conviction *belongs* to strength, to the *ability* to open one's eyes freely. . . . The great passion of a sceptic, the basis and power of his being, which is more enlightened and more despotic than he is himself, enlists all his intellect into its service; it makes him unscrupulous; it even gives him the courage to employ unholy means; in certain circumstances it even allows him convictions. Conviction as a *means:* much is achieved merely by means of a conviction. Great passion makes use of and consumes convictions, it does not submit to them—it knows that it is a sovereign power. Conversely; the need of faith, of anything either absolutely affirmative or negative, Carlylism (if I may be allowed this expression), is the need of *weakness*. The man of beliefs, the "believer" of every sort and condition, is necessarily a dependent man; he is one who cannot regard *himself* as an aim, who cannot postulate aims from the promptings of his own heart. The "believer" does not belong to himself, he can be only a means, he must be *used up*, he is in need of someone who uses him up. His instinct accords the highest honor to a morality of self-abnegation: everything in him, his prudence, his experience, his vanity, persuade him to adopt this morality. Every sort of belief is in itself an expression of self-denial, of self-estrangement. . . . If one considers how necessary a regulating code of conduct is to the majority of people, a code of conduct which constrains them and fixes them from outside; and how control, or in a higher sense, *slavery*, is the only and ultimate condition under which the weak-willed man, and especially woman, flourish; one also understands conviction, "faith." The man of conviction finds in the latter his *backbone*. To be *blind* to many things, to be impartial about nothing, to belong always to a particular side, to hold a strict and necessary point of view in all matters of values—these are the only conditions under which such a man can survive at all. But all this is the reverse of, the *antagonist* of, the truthful man, of truth. . . . The believer is not at liberty to have a conscience for the question "true" and "untrue": to be upright on *this* point would mean his immediate downfall. The pathological limitations of his standpoint convert the convinced man into the fanatic—Savonarola, Luther Rousseau, Robespierre, Saint-Simon, these are the reverse type of the strong spirit that has become *free*. But the grandiose poses of these *morbid* spirits, of these epileptics of ideas, exercise an influence over the masses, fanatics are picturesque, mankind prefers to look at poses than to listen to reason.

55

One step further in the psychology of conviction of "faith." It is already sometime since I first thought of considering whether convictions were not perhaps more dangerous enemies of truth than lies ("Human All-too-Human," Part I, Aphs. 54 and 483). Now I would fain put the decisive question: is there any difference at all between a lie and a conviction? All the world believes that there is, but what in Heaven's name does not all the world believe! Every conviction has its history, its preliminary stages, its period of groping and of mistakes: it becomes a conviction only after it has *not* been one for a long time, only after it has *scarcely* been one for a long time. What? Might not falsehood be the embryonic form of conviction? At times all that is required is a change of personality: very often what was a lie in the father becomes a conviction in the son. I call a lie, to refuse to see something that one sees, to refuse to see it exactly *as* one sees it: whether a lie is perpetrated before witnesses or not is beside the point. The most common sort of lie is the one uttered to one's self; to lie to others is relatively exceptional. Now this refusal to see what one sees, this refusal to see a thing exactly as one sees it, is almost the first condition for all those who belong to a *party* in any sense whatsoever: the man who belongs to a party perforce becomes a liar. German historians, for instance, are convinced that Rome stood for despotism, whereas the Teutons introduced the spirit of freedom into the world: what difference is there between this conviction and a lie? After this is it to be wondered at, that all parties, including German historians, instinctively adopt the grandiloquent phraseology of morality, that morality almost owes its *survival* to the fact that the man who belongs to a party, no matter what it may be, is in need of morality every moment? "This is our conviction: we confess it to the whole world, we live and die for it, let us respect everything that has a conviction!"—I have actually heard antisemites speak in this way. On the contrary, my dear sirs! An antisemite does not become the least bit more respectable because he lies on principle. . . . Priests, who in such matters are more subtle, and who perfectly understand the objection to which the idea of a conviction lies open—that is to say of a falsehood which is perpetrated on principle *because* it serves a purpose, borrowed from the Jews the prudent measure of setting the concept "God," "Will of God," "Revelation of God," at this place. Kant, too, with his categorical imperative, was on the same road: this was his *practical* reason. There are some questions in which it is *not* given to man to decide between true and false; all the principal questions, all the principal problems of value, stand beyond human reason. . . . To

THE ANTICHRIST ❧ 63

comprehend the limits of reason—this alone is genuine philosophy. For what purpose did God give man revelation? Would God have done anything superfluous? Man cannot of his own accord know what is good and what is evil, that is why God taught man his will. . . . Moral: the priest does *not* lie, such questions as "truth" or "falseness" have nothing to do with the things concerning which the priest speaks; such things do not allow of lying. For, in order to lie, it would be necessary to know *what* is true in this respect. But that is precisely what man cannot know: hence the priest is only the mouthpiece of God. This sort of sacerdotal syllogism is by no means exclusively Judaic or Christian; the right to lie and the *prudent measure* of "revelation" belongs to the priestly type, whether of decadent periods or of Pagan times (—Pagans are all those who say yea to life, and to whom "God" is the word for the great yea to all things). The "law," the "will of God," the "holy book," and inspiration. All these things are merely words for the conditions under which the priest attains to power, and with which he maintains his power, these concepts are to be found at the base of all sacerdotal organisations, of all priestly or philosophical and ecclesiastical governments. The "holy lie," which is common to Confucius, to the *Law-Book of Manu*, to Muhamed, and to the Christian church, is not even absent in Plato. "Truth is here"; this phrase means, wherever it is uttered: *the priest lies*. . . .

56

After all, the question is, to what *end* are falsehoods perpetrated? The fact that, in Christianity, "holy" ends are entirely absent, constitutes *my* objection to the means it employs. Its ends are only *bad* ends: the poisoning, the calumniation and the denial of life, the contempt of the body, the degradation and self-pollution of man by virtue of the concept sin, consequently its means are bad as well. My feelings are quite the reverse when I read the *Law-Book of Manu*, an incomparably superior and more intellectual work, which it would be a sin against the *spirit* even to *mention* in the same breath with the Bible. You will guess immediately why: it has a genuine philosophy behind it, *in* it, not merely an evil-smelling Jewish distillation of Rabbinism and superstition, it gives something to chew even to the most fastidious psychologist. And, *not* to forget the most important point of all, it is fundamentally different from every kind of Bible: by means of it the *noble classes*, the philosophers and the warriors guard and guide the masses; it is replete with noble values, it is filled with a feeling of perfection, with a saying of yea to life, and a triumphant sense of well-being in regard to itself and to life, the sun shines upon the whole book. All those things which Christianity smothers with its bottomless vulgarity: procreation, woman, marriage, are here treated with earnestness, with reverence, with love and confidence. How can one possibly place in the hands of children and women, a book that contains those vile words: "to avoid fornication, let every man have his own wife, and let every woman have her own husband . . . it is better to marry than to burn."[11] And is it decent to be a Christian so long as the very origin of man is Christianised, that is to say, befouled, by the idea of the *immaculata conceptio?* . . . I know of no book in which so many delicate and kindly things are said to woman, as in the *Law-Book of Manu*; these old grey-beards and saints have a manner of being gallant to women which, perhaps, cannot be surpassed. "The mouth of a woman," says Manu on one occasion," the breast of a maiden, the prayer of a child, and the smoke of the sacrifice, are always pure." Elsewhere he says: "there is nothing purer than the light of the sun, the shadow cast by a cow, air, water, fire and the breath of a maiden." And finally—perhaps this is also a holy lie: "all the openings of the body above the navel are pure, all those below the navel are impure. Only in a maiden is the whole body pure."

57

The unholiness of Christian means is caught *in flagranti*, if only the end aspired to by Christianity be compared with that of the *Law-Book of Manu*; if only these two utterly opposed aims be put under a strong light. The critic of Christianity simply cannot avoid making Christianity *contemptible*. A law-book like that of Manu comes into being like every good law-book: it epitomises the experience, the precautionary measures, and the experimental morality of long ages, it settles things definitely, it no longer creates. The prerequisite for a codification of this kind, is the recognition of the fact that the means which procure authority for a *truth* to which it has cost both time and great pains to attain, are fundamentally different from those with which that same truth would be proved. A law-book never relates the utility, the reasons, the preliminary casuistry, of a law: for it would be precisely in this way that it would forfeit its imperative tone, the "thou shalt," the first condition of its being obeyed. The problem lies exactly in this. At a certain stage in the development of a people, the most far-seeing class within it (that is to say, the class that sees farthest backwards and forwards), declares the experience of how its fellow-creatures ought to live—i.e., *can* live—to be finally settled. Its object is, to reap as rich and as complete a harvest as possible, in return for the ages of experiment and *terrible* experience it has traversed. Consequently, that which has to be avoided, above all, is any further experimentation, the continuation of the state when values are still fluid, the testing, choosing, and criticising of values *in infinitum*. Against all this a double wall is built up: in the first place, *Revelation*, which is the assumption that the rationale of every law is not human in its origin, that it was not sought and found after ages of error, but that it is divine in its origin, completely and utterly without a history, a gift, a miracle, a mere communication. . . . And secondly, *tradition*, which is the assumption that the law has obtained since the most primeval times, that it is impious and a crime against one's ancestors to attempt to doubt it. The authority of law is established on the principles: God *gave* it, the ancestors *lived* it. The superior reason of such a procedure lies in the intention to draw consciousness off step by step from that mode of life which has been recognised as correct (i.e., *proved* after enormous and carefully examined experience), so that perfect automatism of the instincts may be attained, this being the only possible basis of all mastery of every kind of perfection in the Art of Life. To draw up a law-book like Manu's, is tantamount to granting a people mastership for the future, perfection for the future, the right to aspire to the highest Art of Life. *To that end it must be made unconscious:* this

is the object of every holy lie. *The order of castes*, the highest, the dominating law, is only the sanction of a *natural order*, of a natural legislation
of the first rank, over which no arbitrary innovation, no "modern idea"
has any power. Every healthy society falls into three distinct types,
which reciprocally condition one another and which gravitate differ-
ently in the physiological sense; and each of these has its own hygiene,
its own sphere of work, its own special feeling of perfection, and its
own mastership. It is Nature, not Manu, that separates from the rest,
those individuals preponderating in intellectual power, those excelling
in muscular strength and temperament, and the third class which is
distinguished neither in one way nor the other, the mediocre, the
latter as the greatest number, the former as the *élite.* The superior
caste—I call them the *fewest*, has, as the perfect caste, the privileges
of the fewest: it devolves upon them to represent happiness, beauty
and goodness on earth. Only the most intellectual men have the right
to beauty, to the beautiful: only in them is goodness not weakness.
*Pulchrum est paucorum hominum:* goodness is a privilege. On the other
hand there is nothing which they should be more strictly forbidden
than repulsive manners or a pessimistic look, a look that makes
everything *seem ugly*, or even indignation at the general aspect of
things. Indignation is the privilege of the Chandala, and so is pessi-
mism. "*The world is perfect*"—that is what the instinct of the most
intellectual says, the yea-saying instinct; "imperfection, every kind of
*inferiority* to us, distance, the pathos of distance, even the Chandala
belongs to this perfection. "The most intellectual men, as the *strongest*
find their happiness where others meet with their ruin: in the labyrinth, in hardness towards themselves and others, in endeavor;
their delight is self-mastery: with them asceticism becomes a second
nature, a need, an instinct They regard a difficult task as their privilege; to play with burdens which crush their fellows is to them a
*recreation.* . . . Knowledge, a form of asceticism. They are the most
honorable kind of men: but that does not prevent them from being
the most cheerful and most gracious. They rule, not because they
will, but because they *are;* they are not at liberty to take a second place.
The second in rank are the guardians of the law, the custodians of
order and of security, the noble warriors, the king, above all, as the

highest formula of the warrior, the judge, and keeper of the law. The second in rank are the executive of the most intellectual, the nearest to them in duty, relieving them of all that is *coarse* in the work of ruling, their retinue, their right hand, their best disciples. In all this, I repeat, there is nothing arbitrary, nothing "artificial," that which is *otherwise* is artificial, by that which is otherwise, nature is put to shame. . . . The order of castes, and the order of rank merely formulates the supreme law of life itself; the differentiation of the three types is necessary for the maintenance of society, and for enabling higher and highest types to be reared, the *inequality* of rights is the only condition of there being rights at all. A right is a privilege. And in his way, each has his privilege. Let us not underestimate the privileges of the *mediocre*. Life always gets harder towards the summit, the cold increases, responsibility increases. A high civilization is a pyramid: it can stand only upon a broad base, its first prerequisite is a strongly and soundly consolidated mediocrity. Handicraft, commerce, agriculture, science, the greater part of art, in a word, the whole range of professional and business callings, is compatible only with mediocre ability and ambition; such pursuits would be out of place among exceptions, the instinct pertaining thereto would oppose not only aristocracy but anarchy as well. The fact that one is publicly useful, a wheel, a function, presupposes a certain natural destiny: it is not *society*, but the only kind of *happiness* of which the great majority are capable, that makes them intelligent machines. For the mediocre it is a joy to be mediocre; in them mastery in one thing, a speciality, is a natural instinct. It would be absolutely unworthy of a profound thinker to see any objection in mediocrity *per se*. For in itself it is the first essential condition under which exceptions are possible; a high culture is determined by it. When the exceptional man treats the mediocre with more tender care than he does himself or his equals, this is not mere courtesy of heart on his part—but simply his *duty*. . . . Whom do I hate most among the rabble of the present day? The socialistic rabble, the Chandala apostles, who undermine the working man's instinct, his happiness and his feeling of contentedness with his insignificant existence, who make him envious, and who teach him revenge. . . . The wrong never lies in unequal rights; it lies in the claim to equal rights. What is *bad?* But I have already replied to this: Everything that proceeds from weakness, envy and *revenge.* The anarchist and the Christian are offspring of the same womb. . . .

58

In point of fact, it matters greatly to what end one lies: whether one preserves or *destroys* by means of falsehood. It is quite justifiable to bracket the *Christian* and the *Anarchist* together: their object, their instinct, is concerned only with destruction. The proof of this proposition can be read quite plainly from history: history spells it with appalling distinctness. Whereas we have just seen a religious legislation, whose object was to render the highest possible means of making life *flourish,* and of making a grand organisation of society, eternal, Christianity found its mission in putting an end to such an organisation, *precisely because life flourishes through it.* In the one case, the net profit to the credit of reason, acquired through long ages of experiment and of insecurity, is applied usefully to the most remote ends, and the harvest, which is as large, as rich and as complete as possible, is reaped and garnered: in the other case, on the contrary, the harvest is *blighted* in a single night. That which stood there, *ære perennius,* the *imperium Romanum,* the most magnificent form of organisation, under difficult conditions, that has ever been achieved, and compared with which everything that preceded, and everything which followed it, is mere patchwork, gimcrackery, and dilettantism, those holy anarchists made it their "piety," to destroy "the world"—that is to say, the *imperium Romanum,* until no two stones were left standing one on the other, until even the Teutons and other clodhoppers were able to become master of it. The Christian and the anarchist are both decadents; they are both incapable of acting in any other way than disintegratingly, poisonously and witheringly, like *blood-suckers;* they are both actuated by an instinct of *mortal hatred* of everything that stands erect, that is great, that is lasting, and that is a guarantee of the future. . . . Christianity was the vampire of the *imperium Romanum,* in a night it shattered the stupendous achievement of the Romans, which was to acquire the territory for a vast civilization which could *bide its time*. Does no one understand this yet? The *imperium Romanum* that we know, and which the history of the Roman province teaches us to know ever more thoroughly, this most admirable work of art on a grand scale, was the beginning, its construction was calculated *to prove* its worth by millenniums, unto this day nothing has ever again been built in this fashion, nor have men even dreamt since of building on this scale *sub specie æterni!* This organisation was sufficiently firm to withstand bad emperors: the accident of personalities must have nothing to do with such matters—the *first* principle of all great architecture. But it was not sufficiently firm to resist the *corruptest* form of corruption, to resist the Christians. . . . These stealthy canker-worms, which under the shadow of night, mist and duplicity, insinuated themselves into the company of every individual, and proceeded to drain him of all seriousness for *real* things, of all his instinct for *realities;* this cowardly, effeminate and sugary gang have step by step alienated all "souls" from this colossal edifice, those valuable, virile, and noble natures who felt that the cause of Rome was their own personal cause, their own personal seriousness, their own personal *pride*. The stealth of the bigot, the secrecy of the conventicle, concepts as black as hell such as the sacrifice of the innocent, the *unio mystica* in the drinking of blood, above all the slowly kindled fire of revenge, of Chandala revenge—such things became master of Rome, the same kind of religion on the pre-existent form of which Epicurus had waged war. One has only to read Lucretius in order to understand what Epicurus combated, *not* Paganism, but "Christianity," that is to say the corruption of souls through the concept of guilt, through the concept of punishment and immortality. He combated the *subterranean* cults, the whole of latent Christianity—to deny immortality was at that time a genuine *deliverance*. And Epicurus had triumphed, every respectable thinker in the Roman Empire was an Epicurean: *then St Paul appeared* . . . St Paul, the Chandala hatred against Rome, against "the world," the Jew, the eternal Jew *par excellence*, become flesh and genius. . . . What he divined was, how, by the help of the small sectarian Christian movement, independent of Judaism, a universal conflagration could be kindled; how, with the symbol of the "God on the Cross," everything submerged, everything secretly insurrectionary, the whole offspring of anarchical intrigues could be gathered together to constitute an enormous power. "For salvation is of the Jews." Christianity is the formula for the supersession, *and* epitomising of all kinds of subterranean cults, that of Osiris, of the Great Mother, of Mithras for example: St Paul's genius consisted in his discovery of this. In this matter his instinct was so certain, that, regardless of doing violence to truth, he laid the ideas by means of which those Chandala religions fascinated, upon the very lips of the "Savior" he had invented, and not only upon his lips, that he *made* out of him something which even a Mithras priest could understand. . . . This was his moment of Damascus: he saw that he had *need* of the belief in immortality in order to depreciate "the world," that the notion of "hell" would become master of Rome, that with a "Beyond" *this life* can be killed. . . . Nihilist and Christian, they rhyme in German, and they do not only rhyme.

59

The whole labor of the ancient world *in vain:* I am at a loss for a word which could express my feelings at something so atrocious. And in view of the fact that its labor was only preparatory, that with adamantine self-consciousness it laid the substructure, alone, to a work which was to last millenniums, the whole *significance* of the ancient world was certainly in vain! . . . What was the use of the Greeks? What was the use of the Romans? All the prerequisites of a learned culture, all the scientific methods already existed, the great and peerless art of reading well had already been established—that indispensable condition to tradition, to culture and to scientific unity; natural science hand in hand with mathematics and mechanics was on the best possible road, the sense for facts, the last and most valuable of all senses, had its schools, and its tradition was already centuries old! Is this understood? Everything *essential* had been discovered to make it possible for work to be begun: methods, and this cannot be said too often, are the essential thing, also the most difficult thing, while they moreover have to wage the longest war against custom and indolence. That which today we have successfully reconquered for ourselves, by dint of unspeakable self-discipline—for in some way or other all of us still have the bad instincts, the Christian instincts, in our body, the impartial eye for reality, the cautious hand, patience and seriousness in the smallest details, complete *upright-ness* in knowledge, all this was already there; it had been there over two thousand years before! And in addition to this there was also that excellent and subtle tact and taste! *Not* in the form of brain drilling! *Not* in the form of "German" culture with the manners of a boor! But incarnate, manifesting itself in men's bearing and in their instinct, in short constituting reality. . . . *All this in vain!* In one night it became merely a memory! The Greeks! The Romans! Instinctive nobility, instinctive taste, methodic research, the genius of organisation and administration, faith, the *will* to the future of mankind, the great *yea* to all things materialised in the *imperium Romanum*, become visible to all the senses, grand style no longer manifested in mere art, but in reality, in truth, in *life*. And buried in a night, not by a natural catastrophe! Not stamped to death by Teutons and other heavy-footed vandals! But destroyed by crafty, stealthy, invisible anæmic vampires! Not conquered, but only drained of blood! . . . The concealed lust of revenge, miserable envy become *master!* Everything wretched, inwardly ailing, and full of ignoble feel-ings, the whole Ghetto-world of souls, was in a trice *uppermost!* One only needs to read anyone of the Christian agitators—St Augustine, for instance, in order to realize, in order to *smell*, what filthy fellows came to the top in this movement. You would deceive yourselves utterly if you supposed that the leaders of the Christian agitation showed any lack of understanding: Ah! They were shrewd, shrewd to the point of holiness were these dear old Fathers of the Church! What they lack is something quite different. Nature neglected them, it forgot to give them a modest dowry of decent, of respectable and of *cleanly* instincts. . . . Between ourselves, they are not even men. If Islam despises Christianity, it is justified a thousand times over; for Islam presupposes men.

60

Christianity destroyed the harvest we might have reaped from the culture of antiquity, later it also destroyed our harvest of the culture of Islam. The wonderful Moorish world of Spanish culture, which in its essence is more closely related to *us*, and which appeals more to our sense and taste than Rome and Greece, was *trampled to death* (I do not say by what kind of feet), why? Because it owed its origin to noble, to manly instincts, because it said yea to life, even that life so full of the rare and refined luxuries of the Moors! . . . Later on the Crusaders waged war upon something before which it would have been more seemly in them to grovel in the dust, a culture, beside which even our Nineteenth Century would seem very poor and very "senile." Of course they wanted booty: the Orient was rich. . . . For goodness' sake let us forget our prejudices! Crusades—superior piracy, that is all! German nobility—that is to say, a Viking nobility at bottom, was in its element in such wars: the Church was only too well aware of how German nobility is to be won. . . . German nobility was always the "Swiss Guard" of the Church, always at the service of all the bad instincts of the Church; but it was *well paid for it all.* . . . Fancy the Church having waged its deadly war upon everything noble on earth, precisely with the help of German swords, German blood and cour- age! A host of painful *questions* might be raised on this point. German nobility scarcely takes a place in the history o higher culture: the reason of this is obvious Christianity, alcohol—the two *great* means of corrup- tion. As a matter of fact, choice ought to be just as much out of the question between Islam and Christianity, as between an Arab and a Jew. The decision is already self-evident; nobody is at liberty to exercise a choice in this matter. A man is either of the Chandala or he is *not.* . . . "War with Rome to the knife! Peace and friendship with Islam": this is what that great free spirit, that genius among German emperors, Frederick the Second, not only felt but also *did.* What? Must a German in the first place be a genius, a free-spirit, in order to have *decent* feelings? I cannot understand how a German was ever able to have *Christian* feelings.

61

Here it is necessary to revive a memory which will be a hundred times more painful to Germans. The Germans have destroyed the last great harvest of culture which was to be garnered for Europe, it destroyed the *Renaissance*. Does anybody at last understand, *will* anybody understand what the Renaissance was? *The transvaluation of Christian values*, the attempt undertaken with all means, all instincts and all genius to make the *opposite* values, the *noble* values triumph. . . . Hitherto there has been only *this* great war: there has never yet been a more decisive question than the Renaissance, *my* question is the question of the Renaissance: there has never been a more fundamental, a more direct and a more severe *attack*, delivered with a whole front upon the centre of the foe. To attack at the decisive quarter, at the very seat of Christianity, and there to place *noble* values on the throne, that is to say, to *introduce* them into the instincts, into the most fundamental needs and desires of those sitting there. . . . I see before me a possibility perfectly magic in its charm and glorious coloring—it seems to me to scintillate with all the quivering grandeur of refined beauty, that there is an art at work within it which is so divine, so infernally divine, that one might seek through millenniums in vain for another such possibility; I see a spectacle so rich in meaning and so wonderfully paradoxical to boot, that it would be enough to make all the gods of Olympus rock with immortal laughter, *Cæsar Borgia as Pope*. . . . Do you understand me?. . . Very well then, this would have been the triumph which *I* alone am longing for today: this would have *swept* Christianity *away!* What happened? A German monk, Luther, came to Rome. This monk, with all the vindictive instincts of an abortive priest in his body, foamed with rage over the Renaissance in Rome. . . . Instead of, with the profoundest gratitude, understanding the vast miracle that had taken place, the overcoming of Christianity at its *headquarters*, the fire of his hate knew only how to draw fresh fuel from this spectacle. A religious man thinks only of himself. Luther saw the corruption of the Papacy when the very reverse stared him in the face: the old corruption, the *peccatum originale*, Christianity *no* longer sat upon the Papal chair! But Life! The triumph of Life! The great yea to all lofty, beautiful and daring things! . . . And Luther reinstated the Church; he attacked it. The Renaissance thus became an event without meaning, a great *in vain!* Ah these Germans, what have they not cost us already! In vain—this has always been the achievement of the Germans. The Reformation, Leibniz, Kant and so-called German philosophy, the Wars of Liberation, the Empire—in each case are in vain for something which had already existed, for something which *cannot be recovered.* . . . I confess it, these Germans are my enemies: I despise every sort of uncleanliness in concepts and valuations in them, every kind of cowardice in the face of every honest yea or nay. For almost one thousand years, now, they have tangled and confused everything they have laid their hands on; they have on their conscience all the half-measures, all the three-eighth measures of which Europe is sick; they also have the most unclean, the most incurable, and the most irrefutable kind of Christianity—Protestantism—on their conscience. . . . If we shall never be able to get rid of Christianity, the *Germans* will be to blame.

62

—With this I will now conclude and pronounce my judgment. I *condemn* Christianity and confront it with the most terrible accusation that an accuser has ever had in his mouth. To my mind it is the greatest of all conceivable corruptions, it has had the will to the last imaginable corruption. The Christian Church allowed, nothing to escape from its corruption; it converted every value into its opposite, every truth into a lie, and every honest impulse into an ignominy of the soul. Let anyone dare to speak to me of its humanitarian blessings! To *abolish* any sort of distress was opposed to its profoundest interests; its very existence depended on states of distress; it created states of distress in order to make itself immortal. . . . The cancer germ of sin, for instance: the Church was the first to enrich mankind with this misery! The "equality of souls before God," this falsehood, this *pretext* for the *rancunes* of all the base-minded, this anarchist bomb of a concept, which has ultimately become the revolution, the modern idea, the principle of decay of the whole of social order, this is *Christian dynamite.* . . . The "humanitarian" blessings of Christianity! To breed a self-contradiction, an art of self-profanation, a will to lie at any price, an aversion, a contempt of all good and honest instincts out of *humanitas!* Is this what you call the blessings of Christianity? Parasitism as the only method of the Church; sucking all the blood, all the love, all the hope of life out of mankind with anæmic and sacred ideals. A "Beyond" as the will to deny all reality; the cross as the trade-mark of the most subterranean form of conspiracy that has ever existed, against health, beauty, well-constitutedness, bravery, intellect, kindliness of soul, *against Life itself.* . . .

This eternal accusation against Christianity I would fain write on all walls, wherever there are walls, I have letters with which I can make even the blind see. . . . I call Christianity the one great curse, the one enormous and innermost perversion, the one great instinct of revenge, for which no means are too venomous, too underhand, too underground and too *petty,* I call it the one immortal blemish of mankind. . . .

And *time* is reckoned from the *dies nefastus* upon which this fatality came into being—from the first day of Christianity! *Why not rather from its last day? From today?* Transvaluation of all Values! . . .

# ENDNOTES

1. The German "*Tüchtigkeit*" has a nobler ring than our word "efficiency." Tr.
2. *Cf.* Disraeli: "But enlightened Europe is not happy. Its existence is a fever which it calls progress. Progress to what?" ("Tancred," Book III., Chap. vii.). Tr.
3. It will be seen from this that in spite of Nietzsche's ruthless criticism of the priests, he draws a sharp distinction between Christianity and the Church. As the latter still contained elements of order, it was more to his taste than the denial of authority characteristic of real Christianity. Tr.
4. "*Reine Thorheit*" in the German text, referring once again to Parsifal. Tr.
5. This applies apparently to Bismarck, the forger of the Ems telegram and a sincere Christian. Tr.
6. An adaptation of Shakespeare's "Well roared, lion" (*Mid. N. D.*, Act 5, Sc. i.), the lion, as is well known, being the symbol for St Mark in Christian literature and Art. Tr.
7. A parody on a line in Schiller's "*Jungfrau von Orleans*" (Act 3, Sc. vi.): "*Mit den Dummheit kämpfen Götter selbst vergebens*" (With stupidity even the gods themselves struggle in vain). Tr.
8. ἔφεξις = Lat. Retentio, Inhibitio (Stephanus, Thesaurus Græcæ Linguæ); therefore: reserve, caution. The Greek Sceptics were also called Ephectics owing to their caution in judging and in concluding from facts. Tr.
9. The following passage from Multatuli will throw light on this passage:

    Father: Behold, my son, how wisely Providence has arranged everything! This bird lays its eggs in its nest and the young will be hatched just about the time when there will be worms and flies with which to feed them. Then they will sing a song of praise in honor of the Creator who overwhelms his creatures with blessings.
    Son: Will the worms join in the song, Dad? Tr.

10. *Thus Spake Zarathustra.* The Priests. Tr.
11. 1 Corinthians vii. 2, 9. Tr.

# SUGGESTED READING

⊸✕⊶

ALLISON, D. B., ED. *The New Nietzsche: Contemporary Styles of Interpretation.* New York: Delta Books, 1977.

CATE, C. *Friedrich Nietzsche.* New York: Overlook Press, 2005.

DANTO, A. *Nietzsche As Philosopher.* New York: Macmillan, 1968.

DIETHE, C. *Nietzsche's Sister and the Will to Power: A Biography of Elisabeth Förster-Nietzsche.* Champaign: University of Illinois Press, 2003.

FUSS, P., AND H. SHAPIRO, EDS. *Nietzsche: A Self-Portrait from His Letters.* Cambridge, MA: Harvard University Press, 1971.

HAYMAN, R. *Nietzsche: A Critical Life.* New York: Penguin Books, 1982.

HOLLINGDALE, H. J. *Nietzsche: The Man and His Philosophy.* Cambridge: Cambridge University Press, 1999.

KAUFMANN, W. *Nietzsche: Philosopher, Psychologist, Antichrist.* 4th ed. Princeton: Princeton University Press, 1974.

KRELL, D. F., AND D. WOOD, EDS. *Exceedingly Nietzsche: Aspects of Contemporary Nietzsche Interpretation.* London: Routledge, 1988.

NEHAMAS, A. *Nietzsche: Life as Literature.* Cambridge, MA: Harvard University Press, 1985.

NIETZSCHE, F. *The Birth of Tragedy and The Case of Wagner.* Trans. by W. Kaufmann. New York: Vintage Books, 1967.

———. *Daybreak: Thoughts on the Prejudices of Morality.* Trans. by R. J. Hollingdale. Cambridge: Cambridge University Press, 1982.

———. *The Gay Science.* Trans. by W. Kaufmann. New York: Vintage Books, 1974.

———. *Thus Spoke Zarathustra.* Contained in *The Portable Nietzsche.* Trans. by W. Kaufmann. New York: The Viking Press, 1976.

———. *Beyond Good and Evil.* Trans. by W. Kaufmann. New York: Vintage Books, 1966.

———. *On the Genealogy of Morals and Ecce Homo.* Trans. by W. Kaufmann. New York: Vintage Books, 1969.

———. *The Will to Power.* Trans. by W. Kaufmann and R. J. Hollingdale. New York: Vintage Books, 1968.

SALOMÉ, L. *Nietzsche.* (Originally published in 1894.) Trans. by S. Mandel. Champaign: University of Illinois Press, 2001.

Look for the following titles, available now from
The Barnes & Noble Library of Essential Reading.

Visit your Barnes & Noble bookstore,
or shop online at *www.bn.com/loer*

## NONFICTION

| | | |
|---|---|---|
| Age of Revolution, The | Winston S. Churchill | 0760768595 |
| Alexander | Theodore Ayrault Dodge | 0760773491 |
| American Democrat, The | James Fenimore Cooper | 0760761981 |
| American Indian Stories | Zitkala-Ša | 0760765502 |
| Ancient Greek Historians, The | J. B. Bury | 0760776350 |
| Ancient History | George Rawlinson | 0760773580 |
| Antichrist, The | Friedrich Nietzsche | 0760777705 |
| Autobiography of Benjamin Franklin, The | Benjamin Franklin | 0760768617 |
| Autobiography of Charles Darwin, The | Charles Darwin | 0760769087 |
| Babylonian Life and History | E. A. Wallis Budge | 0760765499 |
| Beyond the Pleasure Principle | Sigmund Freud | 0760774919 |
| Birth of Britain, The | Winston S. Churchill | 0760768579 |
| Boots and Saddles | Elizabeth B. Custer | 076077370X |
| Characters and Events of Roman History | Guglielmo Ferrero | 0760765928 |
| Chemical History of a Candle, The | Michael Faraday | 0760765227 |
| Civil War, The | Julius Caesar | 0760768943 |
| Common Law, The | Oliver Wendell Holmes | 0760754985 |
| Confessions | Jean-Jacques Rousseau | 0760773599 |
| Conquest of Gaul, The | Julius Caesar | 0760768951 |
| Consolation of Philosophy, The | Boethius | 0760769796 |
| Conversations with Socrates | Xenophon | 0760770441 |

| | | |
|---|---|---|
| Tragic Sense of Life | Miguel de Unamuno | 0760777764 |
| Travels of Marco Polo, The | Marco Polo | 0760765898 |
| Treatise Concerning the Principles of Human Knowledge, A | George Berkeley | 0760777691 |
| Treatise of Human Nature, A | David Hume | 0760771723 |
| Trial and Death of Socrates, The | Plato | 0760762007 |
| Up From Slavery | Booker T. Washington | 0760752346 |
| Utilitarianism | William James | 0760771758 |
| Vindication of the Rights of Woman, A | Mary Wollstonecraft | 0760754942 |
| Violin Playing As I Teach It | Leopold Auer | 0760749914 |
| Voyage of the *Beagle*, The | Charles Darwin | 0760754969 |
| Wealth of Nations, The | Adam Smith | 0760757615 |
| Wilderness Hunter, The | Theodore Roosevelt | 0760756031 |
| Will to Believe and Human Immortality, The | William James | 0760770190 |
| Will to Power, The | Friedrich Nietzsche | 0760777772 |
| Worst Journey in the World, The | Aspley Cherry-Garrard | 0760757593 |
| You Know Me Al | Ring W. Lardner | 0760758336 |

THE BARNES & NOBLE
LIBRARY OF ESSENTIAL READING

This newly developed series has been established to provide affordable access to books of literary, academic, and historic value—works of both well-known writers and those who deserve to be rediscovered. Selected and introduced by scholars and specialists with an intimate knowledge of the works, these volumes present complete, original texts in a modern, readable typeface—welcoming a new generation of readers to influential and important books of the past. With more than 100 titles already in print and more than 100 forthcoming, the Library of Essential Reading offers an unrivaled variety of thought, scholarship, and entertainment. Best of all, these handsome and durable paperbacks are priced to be exceptionally affordable. For a full list of titles, visit *www.bn.com/loer*.